How To Pa
the Written Driv

Also available by Peter Russell
from Bloomsbury Publishing plc

**10 Main Reasons for Failing the Driving Test –
and how to avoid them**
ISBN: 0 7475 1628 6

**10 Important Things Your Driving Instructor Never Taught You –
To Make You a Better Driver**
ISBN: 0 7475 2501 3

How to Pass
the Written Driving Test

PETER RUSSELL

BLOOMSBURY

The information in this book was correct to the best of the editor's and publisher's
belief at the time of going to press. While no responsibility can be accepted for
errors and omissions, the editor and publisher would welcome corrections and
suggestions for material to include in subsequent editions of this book.

First published in 1996 by
Bloomsbury Publishing plc
2 Soho Square
London, W1V 6HB

A copy of the CIP entry for this book is available from the British Library

ISBN 0 7475 2500 5

10 9 8 7 6 5 4 3 2 1

Designed by Planet X
Typeset by Hewer Text Composition Services, Edinburgh
Printed and bound in Britain by Clays Ltd., St Ives plc

Contents

Foreword

The details of the Driving Standards Agency's Written Theory Test

The test will consist of one out of twenty possible test papers, containing thirty-five questions, with a further five possible LGV and PCV tests consisting of twenty-five questions per paper. The questions will be multiple-choice, with a question and four answers. Normally one will be correct, with three distractors, although a few (indicated in the question) will have two correct answers and two wrong ones. The correct answers will be marked in pencil in a bracket and then optically read by computer without the need for a human examiner. The test will cover the whole range of the DSA's examination syllabus, shown on page 147. Candidates will have to score more than twenty-six to pass. Candidates will be allowed at least forty minutes for the written test.

The contract to administer the new written theory driving test has been awarded to DriveSafe Services Limited. This is a joint venture company comprising a partnership of Capita Group plc and JHP Group Limited. Capita is a management services group, and the JHP Group claim to be one of the largest educational training and business services in the country and is based in Coventry.

All the questions are prepared and tested by the National Foundation for Educational Research, with the assistance of a team of driving examiners. DriveSafe will print and distribute the papers and keep them secure. It will also collect and bank the money, conduct and invigilate the tests, mark the papers, send out the results (usually within about two weeks), and keep all the results and details on file.

Learners will not be allowed to gain their full driving licence until both parts of the test have been passed within a two-year period. For the first six months of the theory test's life, until the end of December 1996, the practical test can be taken first. If anyone passed the practical test but is unable to pass the theory test within six months they have to start again. From 1 January 1997 the theory test must be taken first. There is no limit on the number of attempts, nor is there any other time restriction between tests.

The Driving Standards Agency will monitor DriveSafe's activities to ensure the tests are conducted fairly and properly. The DSA has carried out a number of trials on some of the questions; so far many of those in use have not been completely suitable – or correct.

There are 139 new Written Test centres available. They are not more than five miles from towns and cities with populations of more than 1,250 people per square kilometre, twenty miles for areas with populations of 100–1,250, and forty miles for those with less than 100.

To take the tests candidates must be at least seventeen years old, and hold a car or motor cycle provisional licence. From 1 January 1997 candidates for the practical test must also possess a written examination pass certificate to apply for it.

The requirements for the theory testing centres have already been laid down. They will be similar to most normal written forms of testing carried out in secure examination conditions. Candidates will be supplied with pencil and eraser, told when to start, be invigilated during the test, given five minutes' warning before the end, and then told to stop writing as the bell announces the end of the test. Candidates will not be allowed to leave the room once they have started the test, and will not be allowed to remove any working materials at the end. Late arrivals may enter and start the examination, but cannot be allowed any extra time to compensate. Candidates who have first languages other than English, such as Welsh, Chinese, Bengali, Gujerati, Hindi, Punjabi, and Urdu are catered for. Those who are dyslexic or deaf, have physical disabilities, or are in wheelchairs, will be given special consideration. The examination can also be given in audio-tape form for special cases.

The results will be given to the DSA within five days, and to the candidates within ten days. The cost of the examination will be determined at a later date, but figures between £13–£15 have been suggested. The pass mark will be reviewed after the current series of trials has been completed.

The DSA has published a book to help candidates which is called

The Complete Theory Test for Cars and Motorcycles. It contains all 600 questions with the correct answers and why. It is not a learning or teaching text book, however, but is intended to give candidates guidelines about what sort of questions the examination will contain.

The car and motor cycle papers were completed early in 1996, and the LGV and PCV papers just afterwards. The 139 locations of the centres will be announced in May and bookings for the first tests commence from 15 May 1996.

Introduction

There has of course always been a driving theory test for learner drivers. Everyone who has gained a driving licence over the past sixty years will know that at the end of the practical test the driving examiner closed his folder, folded his arms, and said: 'Thank you. That concludes the practical part of the driving test. Switch of your engine, please, and I would like to ask you some questions on the Highway Code and other motoring matters.' Some indication of the real value of this theory test can be given by the many candidates who actually thought the driving examiner said '. . . some questions on the Highway Code not that it matters'! Many examiners would agree. They were then required to ask five questions which required simple answers and show six road and traffic signs which needed to be identified.

There were very many weaknesses in this method of testing a candidate's knowledge of the theoretical side of driving. When examiners received their initial training they were issued with a list of 100 suggested questions, and they were required to write a few of their own as well. They were also issued with a blue booklet (called the DT5), containing forty-eight pictures of road and traffic signs which they used for the road sign test. However the supervision system which driving examiners are subjected to always meant that they were unlikely to produce any really searching or convoluted questions. Most of them played safe and selected the same questions for every test they ever conducted, and instructors were able to guess correctly which ones would be asked. Perhaps the worst feature was that regardless of the answer given by the candidate the examiner always responded with one of two stock phases: 'Thank you', or 'I see', They were not allowed to give any indication to the candidate whether the answer was correct or not, indeed they were not allowed to give any impression of right or wrong, but in truth it made no difference to the test result, so the whole basis of the theory test was a bit of a farce.

The examiners' guidelines for the conduct of the test and on which the result was based were quite simple. If during the drive no serious or dangerous driving faults were committed, then the candidate passed. Even if they answered all their questions wrongly, provided they had done nothing on the test to cause the examiner to put a cross or a 'D' on the marking sheet, they passed. On the other hand if they drove in absolute safety for most of the test, but during a single momentary aberration they failed to stop the wheels at a halt or stop line, then irrespective of their impeccable knowledge of the contents of the Highway Code and of other motoring matters, they failed.

For more than twenty years as Head of Training at the British School of Motoring and as General Secretary of both the Motor Schools Association and the Driving Instructor Association I offered to pay the re-test fee for any candidate who failed their driving test solely on the Highway Code section. During the whole of that time no one ever produced to me a genuine failure form with the heading 'Knowledge of the Highway Code' as the only item marked, and I never had to pay up.

Since 1991 driving examiners have been required to be more user friendly to their customers. This has not always been welcomed by examiners. Indeed many hated the thought that customers might see it as a chance for a discussion, which it was not. Using first names, a post-test explanation of the faults, and giving candidates a copy of the examiner's actual marking sheet, make the test less frightening for many candidates. The general benefit is that test candidates are a bit more relaxed, although the marking system and the actual require-ments to pass, have not changed, and the fact remains that the British driving test is still a daunting prospect. The knowledge that all candidates will now have to take a written theoretical driving test as well as a practical one will not make it any less so. There is only one way to make taking any test easier and that is to know that none of the questions or practical skills tested will be difficult to answer or cope with. Proper preparation is needed, and is the only way to make sure you can pass any examination.

The reason for the current changes to the ways the test is conducted has very little to do with the Driving Standards Agency's aim to make the test more user friendly, however, but is the direct result of the First and Second European Directives on the Harmonization of Driver Licensing, Driver Testing and Driver Training in the European Union, originally published in 1980 and amended on a number of occasions since. Driving licences across Europe were standardized (with the exception of the lack of a photograph on British versions) between 1983 and 1986. The implementation of standardization of testing has taken longer to bring about, because there were so many different approaches to the way tests were conducted in all the member states. Some tests were very strict, other required very little more than driving a hundred metres or so.

The EU Directives laid down a fairly comprehensive syllabus of testing which must be adhered to by all member countries of the EU. Although Britain's practical test has always been considered relatively adequate, we were always the odd country out because we had no written theory test. Most of the others, like Germany, France, Holland and Denmark, had very comprehensive theory tests which could only be taken after attending properly structured theory training programmes. This structured training is where the main difference will be felt in the next few years. When the Department of Transport first published the new British recommended syllabus for learning to drive, based on the EU Directives, in 1989, the contents were laid out in a relatively logical learning sequence. By the time it had got round to realizing how much of it was theoretically based, instead of just what was required to be examined during the practical test, it apparently lost track of what it was trying to achieve: now it has abrogated all responsibility for the conduct of the test and contracted out all the various stages of the theory test.

Theory Testing in Britain

The Department of Transport does have a limited background of traditional theory testing already. For the past thirty years or so all driving examiners and approved driving instructors have had to answer choice questions to get through their own basic examinations to become examiners or instructors. In each case their own examination consisted of 100 questions with only three possible answers. When you are asked a question with three possible answers you can score 33% by answering (a) for each one; with a pass mark of eighty-five the guess factor in this test was quite predominant. The pass mark for multiple-choice examinations has to be set relatively high, and this guess factor was also taken into account in the DSA's instructors' examinations, where the 100 questions are split into four bands of twenty-five. It is necessary to score at least twenty marks out of twenty-five in each of the four bands, which means that it is possible to score 94% and yet still fail. Obviously the range of questions driving examiners and instructors are asked is much wider than that for new drivers, but the principles of testing must remain the same regardless of the level of examination, and in fact the written theory tests for driving examiners and instructors has been changed to the style of the new learner drivers' theory test.

The initial developments for the learner driver theory test were based on the use of computers, with the candidates using keys and touch pads to select the correct answers. Unfortunately not enough time was allowed for the proper preparation of the material and the trials failed miserably. Quite a large proportion of the new theory test is geared around the driver's alertness towards other road users and awareness of danger potential around them. The trials for these using video inserts on a computer screen did not allow candidates to be tested fairly; the slow would only just have made it, whereas the quick were penalized for noting the onset of hazards too soon! Those candidates who hit the answer button at random – without even looking at the screen – were more likely to pass than those who watched the traffic scene change, were quickly aware of potential danger, and then pressed their buttons before the computer expected them to do so. Such is the intelligence of machines. As a result of these malfunctions, and due to the lack of time available for the DSA to meet the necessary deadlines, the next few years will see a written examination using a pen or pencil.

When to prepare for the written theory test

For new learner drivers reading this book in conjunction with taking practical lessons, you should study the first three chapters and then begin your in-car lessons. The ideal time to start to take practical lessons is probably about one third of the way through your theory training. There is no questions of the theory training replacing any of the practical experience of being behind the wheel, but it is important that time is not wasted during your expensive in-car lessons learning things which can be much more easily learned at home or in the classroom.

> **Learning to drive involves three aspects:**
>
> **Skill;   Knowledge; and Attitude.**
>
> Sometimes called
>
> **Psychomotor; Cognitive;   and Effective.**

The **skill** aspects involve learning how to operate the various controls, especially such things as the coordination of accelerator, clutch, and the handbrake when moving off. These will always need to be learned, practised, and a high degree of competence achieved by practical application. However a great deal of background **knowledge** will be helpful even with the practical skills needed to drive a car competently. Other aspects, such as **attitude**, concerning pure knowledge and affecting driver behaviour, can be learned much more intensely through classroom training and private study.

It is these parts of learning to drive which are concentrated on in this book. You can learn to absorb the knowledge needed, and you can develop and improve the correct attitudes towards your own abilities and other road users' with proper guidance, and this book is the best way to do it.

How to prepare for the written theory test using this book

Awareness and alertness in identifying and avoiding risk requires a combination of skill, knowledge, and attitude which needs to be fine tuned by a professional teacher. For many drivers on the road that particular lesson was learned from the most expensive teacher of all – experience – and unfortunately not all drivers survive to learn from this experience, which is why it is essential that new drivers take professional guidance even before they ever get behind a wheel.

Government statistics have proved that although young and new drivers are only 10% of the nations' drivers, they are involved in well over 20% of road accidents, injuries, and deaths. It is not enough to know that seat-belts and other safety equipment now built into vehicles can save lives in an accident. It is avoiding accidents that saves the most lives.

New drivers must be fully aware of the need for alertness at all times, develop correct attitudes towards others, know and make allowances for impairment both for themselves and for others. They must know the main cause of accidents – following too closely – and realize the effects on their braking distance of bad weather and other factors. They must understand and appreciate what risk factors exist and how they can change at any time. They need to develop perception and judgement and decision-making skills in the context of all that is around them.

New drivers of motor cycles and cars need to realize from the very beginning the different problems that drivers of other types of vehicles have. It is not enough to be able to turn right and left safely, they need to realize that other vehicles are not always able to follow the same path when turning that a car or bike can, and that in bad weather conditions all road users are more at risk. Tolerance for others and for changes to road and traffic conditions is vital.

Although new drivers are not allowed to take lessons on motorways whilst they are still L drivers, they should still seek professional advice and guidance after their driving tests to prepare themselves properly for all road conditions. This may mean additional training on motorways, at night, in bad and awkward weather situations, and possibly in off-road parking practice. New drivers must recognize and understand all the road and traffic signs, and be aware of all regulations which may affect them in their day to day activities.

If they intend to own their own car at some time, they need to understand the necessary documentation and regulations which will apply to them. Even if they never want to buy their own car, they must still understand the responsibilities which they assume as persons in charge of a vehicle.

Although the intention is always to avoid accidents, it is a fact of life that they do happen. Drivers must be aware of their responsibilities, both in law and morally, to those who are involved in any accident. If they can assist in any way they should know what to do. If they cannot do anything positive to help, and they are not involved, then they must know to get out of the way to allow those who are doing something room and space to do it. Rubber-necking is an even greater danger.

Finally, drivers must always be aware of their responsibilities to understand enough about the mechanical principles of their vehicles to detect any mechanical faults or defaults which might affect their safety or others'. This also means they must be aware of environmental and safety features built into most cars these days.

How to Pass the Written Driving Test

There are many things you must know even before you get behind the wheel for your first practical driving lesson.

Training is needed, and questions will be asked about everything covered in this chapter.

1. How you get your provisional driving licence

Driving licences are applied for on form DL1, available from any post office, and sent off to DVLC, Swansea SA99 1BN. The current fee for a provisional driving licence covers the issue of all licences until you reach the age of seventy. (However, as photographs will be required on driving licences, this rule may change in the near future. There is no doubt that it will be new drivers who get photographs first.) When you reach seventy you will need to re-apply every three years. Licences can continue to be renewed every three years provided the driver's health and physical condition allows them to drive safely. If there is any doubt, a doctor's confirmation is required to state that the holder is fit and still safe to drive.

The minimum age for holding a provisional car driving licence is seventeen years, but the licence can be applied for up to two months beforehand if necessary, so that driving lessons can start on the driver's seventeenth birthday. This first, provisional licence is an important one, because you cannot drive until you have received – *and signed* – your provisional driving licence. Once you hold any category of licence it acts as a provisional for any other category of vehicle except vocational (categories C, D, E). So if you ride a scooter or moped and hold a licence this also acts as a provisional for a motor car. Every driving licence must be signed immediately you receive it.

Youngsters who are disabled, and in receipt of a mobility allowance for that disability, are allowed to start their driving lessons on their sixteenth birthday.

There are strict controls over the use of provisional driving licences. Proper L plates must be displayed whenever a learner is driving or riding. Motor-cycle learners must also comply with the Compulsory Basic Training regulations before they are allowed to ride on the road. If you are learning to drive a motor car, a requirement of the provisional driving licence is that you must be accompanied by a supervising driver at all times. The supervisor must have held a full licence in the same category for at least three years and be twenty-one or over.

FACT FILE

Driving licences are issued for life; but they need to be renewed every three years from the age of seventy.

No doctor's certificate is needed if the driver is in good health.

If there is any doubt a certificate may need to be obtained.

A list of approved doctors willing to carry out this certification is held by the Driver and Vehicle Licensing Agency, Swansea.

A driving licence is not legal until it has been signed.

Q What is the minimum age at which you can drive a motor car on the road?

A Seventeen, unless you are in receipt of mobility allowance.

Q Can you drive a car if your licence has not yet been received from Swansea?

A You cannot drive until you have received and signed your driving licence.

Q If you suffer from a physical or mental disability likely to last three months or less do you need to surrender your driving licence?

A   No; but you must never drive if you are unable to maintain full control over the vehicle, or if your health interferes with your driving abilities.

Q   If you suffer from a physical or mental disability which is likely to last more than three months do you need to surrender your driving licence?

A   Yes, if you are likely to be unable or unfit to drive through injury, illness, or disability illness, you must inform Swansea and you will not be allowed to drive.

Q   Do you need to inform DVLA if you change your name or address?

A   Yes. It is an offence not to do so.

2. Registration document, Form V5, which covers driving or owning a motor vehicle.

If you actually own the car you are driving then you have to accept responsibility for everything connected with the vehicle. When you learn to drive with a driving school, or in an instructor's own car, then you can take it for granted that you have their permission to drive, although you still need to read the small print in any conditions of service they may give with their driving lessons. If you are borrowing the car – especially from a member of the family or a friend – you need to be sure that you have their permission to drive, and that they know you are a learner driver. You also need to be extra careful about the condition of the vehicle and that it is lawful to drive.

You need to be sure that you know exactly what insurance cover exists on the car whilst you are driving or in charge of it. The law does not make any allowances for the fact that you are new to driving and you don't hold a full driving licence. In law you are responsible for the condition of the car, and for anything that happens to it, or is caused by it whilst you are driving or in charge of it.

FACT FILE

The registration document is often called the car's log book but is officially known as a Form V5.

Although it gives the name of the registered keeper, this does not mean they actually own it; it may be owned by a finance company.

If you buy a car you will receive the updated registration form with your name and address on it. Check that the details are correct. Although this is not proof of ownership it does mean you are responsible for all who drive it, and for any incidents in which the vehicle is involved.

It is an offence to fail to notify DVLA of change of ownership; and it may involve you in paying for someone else's misdemeanours.

Q   Who is responsible in law for giving details of who was driving a vehicle at any particular time?

A   The registered keeper of the vehicle.

Q   Who is responsible for sending the log book to DVLA when you buy a second-hand car?

A   Both the seller and the buyer should send off their respective portions of the document.

Q   Is it an offence not to send off the registration document when selling a car?

A   It is an offence, and pretty stupid too. You can be fined for someone else's bad driving or parking offences.

Q   Do you need the owner's permission to drive their car when taking driving lessons?

A   Yes; you must always check that the owner – or the registered keeper – of the vehicle you are driving has given permission.

Q   Where can you renew the tax disc for your car?

A   At most large post offices and vehicle taxation offices.

Q   What documents do you need to take with you when you tax your vehicle?

A   The renewal form, the insurance certificate, a valid MOT certificate if the vehicle is more than three years old, and the fee.

Q Can you show a photocopy of your insurance certificate?

A No, a photocopy is not allowed, because they are easy to change or forge.

3. The tax disc

As the owner of the vehicle you must ensure that it is properly taxed and that the tax disc is displayed. Tax discs can be obtained from most post offices but you have to show the renewal certificate (which is automatically sent to the registered keeper of the vehicle in the month prior to re-registration), a valid certificate of insurance, and an MOT certificate where appropriate. In all cases the fee must be paid. Vehicles more than twenty-five years old do not need to pay a fee but must still display an exemption disc.

FACT FILE

The tax disc must be displayed in the top left-hand corner of the windscreen facing out or the bottom left-hand corner, which is the more usual place. Anywhere else is not legally correct.

The offence of failing to display can be committed even if the vehicle is taxed – if the licence cannot readily be seen by a police officer from a position ahead of the vehicle just over 1 metre (3 feet) above ground level.

Q Why must the tax disc be displayed in the left-hand side of the window?

A So that a police officer can readily see it at any time.

Q If the tax disc has fallen on the floor is this an offence?

A Yes, failing to display a disc is a separate offence from not having one.

Q Am I allowed fourteen days' grace if my tax disc has expired?

A No. Police officers often take a note of vehicles with out of date or missing tax discs in the first fourteen days of each month, but do not normally prosecute unless the vehicle is not taxed by then.

Q Can I get a refund for my tax disc when I sell the car?

A Yes, but only for whole months. Send the disc back to the regional tax office.

Q My car is only used once a month, do I have to pay tax for the whole year?

A Yes, it is an offence to have a vehicle on the road if it is not taxed.

Q My vehicle is broken down, and I leave it outside my house. Need it be taxed?

A Yes, all vehicles, with a few exemptions, on a public road must be taxed.

Q Which vehicles are exempt from paying Excise duty?

A Those over twenty-five years old, and MOD vehicles.

4. The MOT vehicle certificate (Form VT20)

Vehicles more than three years old need to be tested every year to ensure that they are fully and properly roadworthy. This does not mean that vehicles newer than three years old do not need to meet the same standards of safety, but after three years they all need to pass this annual inspection to make sure that they reach the minimum standards. The test covers a whole range of items, and each driver needs to know what they are and how they can be checked visually on a regular basis.

FACT FILE

1. All vehicles on the roads have to be registered with the Driver and Vehicle Licensing Agency, at Swansea.

2. The initial registration is done by the manufacturer, distributor, or garage, who is first to sell the car to be used on the roads.

3. Subsequent taxation and licensing is required at six-monthly or twelve-monthly intervals by the registered keeper at that time.

4. All vehicles over three years old must be certified road worthy by an MOT licensed garage or mechanic.

The headings of items tested in the Annual vehicle MOT test include: lighting equipment; steering and suspension; brakes; tyres and wheels; seat-belts; and general.

The individual items listed under 'general' include:

the driver's view; horn; exhaust system and emissions; the general vehicle condition; mirrors; fuel system; registration plates and VIN numbers; the speedometer, driving controls, and windscreens.

Details of how you are able to check test them yourself are included later in this book. (See page 42)

Q   What vehicles require a certificate of roadworthiness from an MOT test?

A   All vehicles first registered, or three years from date of manufacture for vehicles used before registration, with exemptions for MOD vehicles.

Q   Am I allowed any period of grace once the certificate has expired?

A   No; but you are allowed to drive the vehicle to keep an appointment for an MOT test, and straight home again if it has failed but is safe.

Q   What items could cause a test-failure?

A   Any item listed above which has an element that does not reach the minimum standard laid down would cause a test failure.

Q   What should I do if my car fails its MOT vehicle test on a minor item such as a wrong fuel filler cap fitted?

A   Replace the offending item, and normally the garage will give you a second test free of charge.

5. ADI certificate and need for its display if professional tuition is being given

Whenever you drive your car on the road whilst holding a provisional driving licence for a motor car you must be supervised. The person supervising you must have held a motor car driving licence for at least three years and must be at least twenty-one years of age. If any money is paid for the training, even for petrol or as part payment for time or vehicle costs, then the person supervising must be an Approved Driving Instructor or a Registered Trainee Instructor. They are also required to show their certificate on the left-hand side of the windscreen. If it is a driving-school car look for it on every lesson. If you take lessons in your own car at any time, ask the instructor to display it whilst you are driving with them in the car with you.

FACT FILE

Approved driving instructors need to take three separate examinations to qualify.

Licensed training instructors also need to have passed the first two examinations, a written theory test and their own driving. They must pass a test of their instructional ability within two years of passing the written test.

Instructors are graded according to their teaching skills by Department of Transport Supervising Examiners: grade 6 is the highest, grade 4 the lowest acceptable standard. Instructors lower than 4 are required to improve or they are taken off the register.

Q   Can I learn to drive in my own car without dual controls?
A   Yes, but you must display proper L plates, and check your insurance, of course.
Q   If a friend offers to teach me to drive should I let them?
A   You can, but you might learn bad habits; it is far better to learn with a professional.
Q   If my friend does teach me, can I pay for their petrol, or other expenses?
A   No, it is an offence to pay money or money's worth for any lessons given.
Q   Should an instructor display an instructional certificate when giving tuition?
A   Yes, it is an offence to give paid instruction unless the certificate is correctly displayed.

Q   Where must the ADI or Trainee certificate to be displayed?
A   Like the tax disc it must be displayed in the front windscreen at the top or bottom, with the photograph and date of expiry clearly visible from the front seats.

6. The minimum insurance requirements and the optimum insurance for your peace of mind

Insurance never means quite what you think it does. 'Comprehensive cover' sounds as if it covers anything that is likely to happen. Actually it only covers you for very specific things. Even driving instructors' own insurance may offer you more limited cover than you think. Make sure that every vehicle you drive is properly insured and that you know what insurance cover you actually have. As the driver of the vehicle, even in a driving-school car, you must know what insurance cover you have. The driving examiner on the practical test will actually ask you. Make sure you know about your insurance and can confirm to the examiner that both you and the examiner are covered by valid insurance.

FACT FILE

There are three main factors covered by insurance: the driver, the vehicle, and the purpose for which the vehicle is being used.

It is an offence to use a vehicle on the roads unless it is properly insured for the purposes for which it is being used.

1. *Third party only* **is the minimum insurance you can normally get. This only covers for any injury or damage you cause to other people, their vehicles, or their property.**

2. *Third party, fire and theft* **additionally covers you for loss of the vehicle, or for damage by fire, but not for damage caused by you or someone else whom you can't trace to get to pay.**

3. *Comprehensive* **insurance normally covers for repairs to your own vehicle as well.**

Q   What is minimum cover required for any vehicle?
A   Death and injury to others in respect of vehicle use; emergency medical treatment; and property damage.
Q   Do I need to carry the insurance policy documents with me in the car?
A   No! You should have the insurance certificate, not the policy, readily available.
Q   Must I have the insurance certificate in the car?
A   No, there is no legal need to have it in the car.
Q   Will professional driving instructors show me their certificates if I ask them?
A   Good professional instructors will show you them automatically. If not you need to ask to see the certificate, or a letter of confirmation if the instructor works on a franchise for a national or large driving school.
Q   Does my insurance cover me to drive other cars?
A   Usually not, but you must read the small print to find out.
Q   What insurance cover can I get when I am learning to drive?
A   You need to shop around whilst you are a learner. The normal insurance is valid only for you and whilst you are driving legally and properly supervised.
Q   Can I learn to drive in my parents' car and be properly insured?
A   You must confirm by asking them that the insurers will give you cover.

7. The medical fitness requirements of a driver

Are you fit to drive? There are a number of things you need to be sure about. Basic fitness is not a problem. The only legal requirement is that you can reach all the controls safely and see correctly. The only medical test which is normally carried out is the eyesight test. You must be able to read a car number plate at 20.5 metres (67 feet). But are you fit to drive?

If you are suffering from a headache, hangover, period pains, or toothache you are scarcely likely to be able to concentrate properly on the driving task. Experienced drivers often find that they have to drive, regardless of any external pains or pressures on them. But novice drivers usually find it much more difficult to cope with the driving task even when all their faculties are working well. If anything else concerns them this is when they are at their most vulnerable.

The reason why new drivers figure so prominently in accident statistics is not hard to see. Their concentration is good – whilst it lasts. But if anything distracts them, they haven't the experience and capability to go on to 'autopilot' and still keep safe. On the other hand some drivers who have permanent disabilities still manage to drive safely and well, in spite of constant pain. The reason? They concentrate solely on controlling their vehicle and the road and traffic situation all the time. And this is the way to cope when you may be feeling just a little bit sluggish or off-colour. Concentrate on what is all around you, and look out for things which may affect you and your intentions.

If you have a permanent disability – of any kind – you may need to confirm with your doctor your basic fitness to drive. Many of my friends, and quite a lot of my ex-pupils, have had some form of disability or another. Not all of them agree that they are 'disabled'. As they themselves say, a disabled ship is one that used to work but now doesn't. But as they know what the term disabled driver has come to mean, and they are usually happy to accept it, we shall still use it here as well. If you have any doubts about what effect your own disability may have there are a number of places where you can have your disabilities properly and professionally assessed.

Disabilities which can debar a driver include those which would prevent the driver maintaining control of the vehicle, or could cause an attack whilst driving. Those which can be ignored or catered for include epilepsy which is being controlled by the use of drugs, or restricted to night-time attacks only, and heart conditions which have been controlled by pacemakers, etc.

Where medication and the use of drugs is used to control illnesses it is essential that drivers get their doctors or other suitably qualified people to confirm that they are capable of controlling a vehicle properly. Many professional driving instructors specialize in training disabled drivers, and some of them have specially adapted vehicles for this purpose.

FACT FILE

Disabilities come under four headings:

Relevant; no driving licence can be issued for relevant disabilities. The main ones are daytime epilepsy and poor eyesight.

Prospective; are of an intermittent or progressive nature which may become relevant in the near future.

Prescribed; are disabilities which have been controlled and the driver is not likely to become a danger.

Temporary; those which will last less than three months.

The responsibility always rests with the driver to be fit to drive. If you are suffering from any form of illness which prevents you giving your full attention to the driving task you should not drive.

Limb disabilities in themselves are not a bar to driving.

All drivers take the same standard practical test. A disabled test merely allows the candidate more time if it is needed.

Any disability declared to an examiner on test may be noted on the driving licence, restricting that driver to certain additional controls or types of vehicle.

Q   Why should I declare any disability I may have when I apply for the practical test?

A   You do so to help yourself. It enables the examiner to ask you questions about your disability in private and allows additional time for the test if needed.

Q   Is deafness a declarable disability?

A   Deafness is no bar to driving. However it helps the examiner to know beforehand.

Q   Should I report a broken leg as a temporary disability?

A   If a doctor says you will be able to drive again within three months you need not. Obviously you should not drive whilst physically impaired in any way.

Q   To whom do I declare a temporary disability?

A   If your disability is likely to last more than three months you should inform the DVLA at Swansea.

Q   I take drugs to control my diabetes; am I likely to be able to learn to drive?

A   In many cases drugs such as insulin enable drivers to cope with driving quite easily. Tell your instructor, of course, and always make sure you are fit to drive.

Q   What adaptations can be fitted to a car to make it easier to drive and still be legal?

A   The most obvious choice is to use an automatic. But you can also have hand controls fitted easily. Other adaptations include electronic joy sticks which enable drivers with a whole variety of impediments to drive safely.

Q   What happens if I have a disability and it gets slightly worse?

A   You have an absolute liability to report any deterioration in any declared disability.

Q   Do disabled drivers take a different driving test to other drivers?

A   No. The test may take longer but this is to give the examiner more time to make allowances that are necessary.

8. The drivers' eyesight requirement and how it is tested

The eyesight test is an absolute one. You must be able to read a number plate at the prescribed distance (20.5 metres, 67 feet) in good daylight. If you need to wear spectacles or contact lenses to read the number plate, you must also wear them all the time when you are driving. The reason for such a simple eyesight test is that it is readily tested not only by driving examiners but also by police officers who may think your eyesight is doubtful.

Eyesight can change with age and illness. Certainly you can expect dramatic changes as you approach middle age. But your eyesight can change at any time, so regular checks are necessary. Once you reach the age of about forty it is essential that you have your eyesight checked professionally every six months or less. Once you have had lenses prescribed for you, you must wear them if you need them for driving and you need to have them checked again at least every year or so.

FACT FILE

The need to monitor and check eyesight regularly is a legal requirement. If you have your eyesight tested by your instructor and you cannot read the number plate at 20.5 metres, you must not continue driving or have any more driving lessons until your eyesight has been checked and corrected.

Bifocal or varifocal lenses can take some getting used to, so if you change your glasses make sure you are comfortable in them before driving. If you suffer from eye-strain at all, do not drive.

Check your night sight too. Some people have no problems in daylight, but cannot see at all well at dusk or in the dark. Do not drive if you suffer from any form of night blindness.

Q   What happens if I tense up and get the eyesight test wrong on my driving test?

A   The examiner will test your eyesight initially slightly beyond the normal distance. If you cannot read it the first time he will measure the distance carefully and then test you again.

Q   What happens if I cannot read it a second time?

A   Normally the examiner will get a colleague to help on the final occasion. The distance will be measured precisely and you must pass this to take the test.

Q   If I fail the eyesight test completely can I drive home?

A   No, you must not drive again until your eyesight has been checked and corrected by an optician.

Q   What happens if the optician says my eyesight is all right?

A   If you cannot read the number plate at the correct distance, in good daylight, you will fail the test and you are still not allowed to drive.

Q   What should I do if I break my glasses or lose my contact lenses whilst out driving in the car?

A   You must not drive with uncorrected eyesight defects. If you cannot read the number plate without your glasses then you must not drive. Carry a spare pair.

9. Vehicle conditions

You must understand the mechanical aspects of your car which have a bearing on road safety. You need to know what daily, weekly, and monthly checks you must carry out on any vehicle you drive, and you need to know why you have to do these checks. Knowing why means you are more likely to want to do them properly.

The reason for regular checks is simple. Your life, and the lives of your passengers, and the lives of the people you will meet every day will depend on the safety of your vehicle. The only way you can be sure your vehicle is as safe as possible is by checking it yourself.

You need to know how the safety of your vehicle can be checked in a prompt and comforting manner. You need to know which bits you can check easily, and which need tools or equipment. You also need to know how to carry out simple routine fault checks without the use of tools. You must be able to identify potential faults and know how to get them repaired safely and effectively. Even such things as an empty screen-washer bottle make your car illegal.

Daily or journey checks
- cleaning all windows, light lenses, and mirrors;

- looking all round the vehicle for any obvious faults;

- filling the screen-washer;

- ensuring that all lights and indicators and the horn are working;

- all warning lights, and after starting the engine that all systems are apparently functioning correctly;

- that the brakes are working by carrying out a brake test while moving.

When carrying out a refuelling stop, it is usually a good time to carry out the following checks: oil level (although this will give a false reading if not done when cold); visual checks of all fluid levels, including power steering if fitted, brakes and clutch levels, battery levels if accessible, and tyre pressures. (Like the oil level, tyre pressures really need to be tested when cold to get a true reading). If the only car you ever drive is your driving instructor's own car, then ask if you can see them carry out a daily check when you have your next driving lesson. A good professional instructor won't need to be asked, because they will know the importance of this matter for you and will be happy to make sure you know not only what to do, but why it is done.

You need to carry out regular checks of everything which can break down, wear out or cause unnecessary trouble later. These checks depend upon how much actual driving you do in your own car and the mileage you cover.

Weekly or monthly check

- look all round and under the vehicle for leaks or puddles;

- clean the vehicle inside and out, and look for any (fresh) rust on the bodywork, since a gram of touch-up paint might save you a whole lot of welding and perhaps a respray later;

- tread depth, looking and feeling for cuts and bulges, and removing any stones or penetrations from the tread;

- tyre pressures, including the spare, and wiper blades to ensure clean and clear operation;

- seat-belts and their free operation;

- twice a year test your anti-freeze level and top up if need be.

FACT FILE

All drivers are responsible in law for every vehicle they drive.

If a defect is discovered, especially one that makes the vehicle illegal, you must not drive it again until the defect has been checked and cleared.

If you are driving an instructors' car and you suspect it is illegal, you must say so.

Indicators should flash between sixty and 120 times a minute.

All lights and lenses should work and be clean.

Tyre pressures should be correct.

And you should not need a great deal of effort to brake or steer the car.

Q   What is meant by daily and weekly checks?
A   They are regular checks made on the important vehicle controls to ensure that the vehicle is as safe as possible.
Q   Why is it necessary for me to know about them?
A   You are responsible for all aspects of the vehicle you are driving, even if you do not own it.
Q   Can I be fined or punished for driving a faulty car not owned by me?
A   Yes, you are legally responsible in law for the vehicle you are driving.
Q   Does this mean that if the car I am driving has faulty tyres I can be held to blame?
A   Yes. You can lose your driving licence as well as being fined or imprisoned for it too.
Q   What does it mean to carry out checks without the use of tools?
A   Many of the daily and regular checks you need to carry out only require a visual check. No one expects you to be a car mechanic, but you must be able to look and feel if everything is safe.
Q   Why is it so important to keep a vehicle in good working order and to carry out checks?
A   Badly maintained vehicles are much more likely to break down or cause accidents.
Q   How can I tell if the brakes are beginning to need replacing?
A   You need to stick to regular servicing schedules and have them carried out properly. That way you'll not be taken by surprise. Routine servicing prevents nasty surprises.
Q   Are my brakes or tyres likely to fail suddenly and without warning?
A   No, very few incidents like this occur. You need to carry out the checks on a regular basis to make sure you are aware of likely faults.
Q   Do I have to be able to repair vehicle faults myself?
A   No, you are not expected to be able to mend them. But you must be able to recognize the need for repairs and make sure they get done by someone who can.

10. How to locate and identify vehicle faults

This includes an understanding of the importance of the correct working and fitment of each of the following. Details of these checks are given on pages 42–46.

- **Steering** Check for any free play on the wheel whilst the car is stationary. If it moves more than half an inch or so, have it checked out. Test also for steering wander when you are driving: the steering wheel should not drag violently one way or another. Check for any power-steering faults if this is fitted, and always avoid turning the wheel whilst you are not moving.

- **Tyres** Look for wear and tear, especially on one side only. This could mean a steering or wheel-adjustment fault. Feel and look for obvious leaks and for cuts, bulges, and splits. Keep an eye on tread depth and be prepared to replace your tyres when the tread is low. Try to fit new tyres on the same axle at the same time.

- **Wheels** Look for cracks and splits, and do not drive a car fitted with odd wheels. Check the wheel nuts are the correct type – especially if you have fitted alloy wheels. Some vehicles, especially old sporty Minis and the like, have often been fitted with wider wheels than originally specified. If you buy a car like this, make sure the wheels are legal and safe.

- **Brakes** Test your brakes often. Get them inspected every time the car is serviced, and find out how many thousands of miles are left on them each time. Get to know what it is like when they are spongy. It is often quite useful to let someone else try your brakes for you at intervals – you get used to your own. You can compare your brakes with other people's cars you may drive. Take care not to let your brake pads wear down, too; if they do you'll stop quicker because the rivets will bite into the discs, and they are very expensive to replace.

- **Lights** Always test your lights before you go out. Don't wait until it is dark before you test them. Make sure all lights work. You can test your brake lights by using a reflecting wall, another car, or a window. Also make sure you don't dazzle other road users; remember that you can easily alter the main beam level by badly loading your car.

- **Reflectors** These are often overlooked, but they must be clean. Remember that your reflectors are all that saves your car in the dark when it is parked on the open road without lights.

- **Indicators** Most indicators have warning lights in the car to let you know if they are not working properly, but still check them, especially the repeater lights at the sides. Check your hazard warning lights occasionally too.

- **Horn** It is an offence to sound the horn whilst you are stationary, but you don't want to sound it when you are driving either. Nevertheless you need to test it out at intervals.

- **Rear-view mirrors** Faulty mirrors, or badly adjusted mirrors, can easily put your life in danger. If you suffer from a broken door mirror get a replacement as soon as possible. A car will fail its MOT test if it has a broken lens, but it means you can't really use them properly too. Never use internal mirrors with bare edges, they are illegal and dangerous.

- **Windscreen wipers** Check that the blades wipe the screen properly, otherwise they can scratch the screen. If they don't clean it properly they can be dangerous and are illegal as well.

- **Windscreen washers** These must be capable of working at all times; keep a check on the reservoir level, and make sure you use proper screen-wash fluid, not plain water or washing-up liquid.

- **Exhaust** Exhaust fumes can kill. Never drive with an estate car or a hatchback's rear door open as fumes can be dragged into the car. You can test the quality of your exhaust fumes by holding a piece of cotton rag or paper tissue about half an inch from the tail pipe when the engine is running. Any deposit should be almost negligible and the rag should not look dirty. If it is oily or very dirty have your engine and exhaust checked. You ought to do this occasionally just to make sure you are not getting near the danger levels of exhaust fumes.

- **Silencer** Once upon a time motor cyclists used to remove the baffles from their silencer boxes to make their bikes sound fast. These days they don't need to. But if you get a hole in your silencer or it gets noisy, get it seen to immediately.

- **Seat-belt operation** Seat-belts save lives; but they can only do so if they work properly. Make sure they run smoothly through your hands, and also that they lock immediately you pull against them tightly.

- **Seat-belt condition** Check that the belts are not frayed, and that they are not likely to slip or snag. If ever your belts are used for a real emergency, get them replaced.

- **Seat-belt fixings** Every now and again you need to check the fixings as well. Certainly do it before you put the car in for a service or an MOT test.

Q How can I test for steering play?

A Sit in the car with the engine off and gently try to turn the wheel. If it moves more than an inch or so without the wheels turning you have too much free play.

Q How often should I do this steering check?

A At least once a month, more if you drive a lot.

Q Are there any other ways I can check for steering wear?

A Look at the front tyre tread. Uneven wear is often caused by steering tracking errors.

Q What is the main cause of steering wear?

A With learner drivers it is usually bumping into the kerb on manoeuvres. If you do bump the kerb any time it is worth while getting your tracking checked.

Q Are there any additional problems associated with power steering?

A Yes, if ever the engine stalls you lose the power to both steering and brakes, making both of them more difficult to handle. Avoid stalling when driving through narrow gaps.

Q What is the minimum tyre tread depth allowed?

A 1.6 millimetres (1/16 inch) across the whole circumference of the tyre.

Q How can I check this easily?

A If in doubt, don't risk it. But you can test a tyre tread with a ten-pence coin; the tread should easily cover the milling and part of the outside lettering.

Q How often should I test the pressures of my tyre?

A Every week is fine. If you find they tend to lose any pressures over a month or so, have them checked for leaks.

Q Can I have a tyre repaired if it gets a puncture?

A Not really, if a tyre is punctured it can never really be trust-worthy again. Get a new one.

Q If I have a puncture can I drive on the flat tyre for a short distance?

A If the tyre is punctured it is illegal to drive on it; but it may be safer to drive on the flat tyre to get to a safe place to change the wheel.

Q Can I have that tyre repaired after driving on it?

A Definitely not. Driving on a punctured tyre wrecks the tyre walls for ever.

Q   What happens if I have a puncture and the spare wheel is not properly inflated?

A   You may have to call out a garage or breakdown organization to help you.

Q   What are Denovo spare tyres?

A   These are special narrow spare tyres that do not take up much room in the boot.

A   Can I drive my car with a Denovo or similar narrow tyre fitted?

A   Yes, but only for short distances (say fifty miles maximum) and at less than fifty mph.

Q   What is the rule about mixing radial and cross-ply tyres?

A   The real answer is never do it. If you must mix them, never do it on the same axle.

Q   How can I test for splits and bulges in my tyres?

A   Run your hands regularly round the back of each tyre feeling for anything strange.

Q   Should I have my wheels balanced when I fit new tyres?

A   Yes, it only costs a little and will keep you safer and let your tyres last longer.

Q   How do they balance wheels and tyres?

A   They take them off the car and spin them on a machine. Then they add little lead weights around the rim to make sure the wheels spin smoothly.

Q   How do I test my brakes?

A   The first way is to sit in the car with the engine off and your foot on the pedal. Then switch on and feel if the brake pedal moves down slightly. This means your power brakes are working.

Q   What other ways are there to test my brakes?

A   At low speeds on a safe, quiet road, take your hands off the wheel and brake firmly. If the car pulls to one side your brakes will need checking. Some garages or brake repair specialists will do this free of charge for you.

Q   Why is it a good idea to let someone else test my brakes for me occasionally?

A   Because you won't notice any gradual changes, whereas they have a straight comparison with other vehicles.

Q   How can I test my handbrake?

A   Pull on it whilst on a hill; it shouldn't make more than six clicks, and it should hold you secure.

Q   If the handbrake doesn't hold on a hill should I leave the car in gear?

A   If the parking brake doesn't work effectively get it fixed.

Q   How can I test my brake-lights?

A   Find a wall or window behind so that you see the red light reflected.

Q   How can I check my headlights on main beam?

A   Switch them on when you are facing a wall or garage door; try dipped and main beam. Try your parking lights too. You can test these by walking round the car.

Q   Can I drive in the daytime if my headlights are not working?

A   No, get them mended as soon as you can. It is illegal to drive with lights not working.

Q   Why are clean reflectors so important?

A   They can still be seen in the dark even when your lights are switched off.

Q   What is the speed which indicators must flash?

A   Between sixty and 120 times per minute. That is once to twice a second.

Q   Does it matter if the lens is broken on my indicators?

A   The colour of your indicator lenses is important. They must not show white to the rear, so broken lenses are illegal.

Q   What happens if my indicators break whilst I am out driving on my own after the test?

A   You must still make every effort to get them mended, especially before it gets dark. Arm signals are not as effective as indicators, and are useless at night.

Q   How should I test the horn?

A   The best way is a light toot every few days, when you know that no one else will be offended or distracted by it. You may be able to sound it properly when out in the country away from other traffic.

Q   How do I test my mirrors to see if they are working properly?

A   Some mirrors these days are electrically operated from the driver's seat. All door mirrors must be able to be operated by the driver whilst inside the vehicle.

Q   If the mirror glass is broken do I need to replace it straight away?

A   Yes, it is an offence to have a broken mirror; but worse than that, you might miss seeing a particular danger.

Q   Is it dangerous not to have your mirrors correctly aligned?

A   It certainly can be. You must have as good a view around your car as possible.

Q What should I be able to see in my door mirrors when they are properly adjusted?

A You should be able to see the sides of the car and as much road as possible with the natural horizon just about midway up the mirror.

Q Is there anything particular I should remember about my door mirrors?

A Yes, they are normally not flat glass so you get a false impression of other road users' speed and distance. They often seem to be further away than they actually are.

Q How can I test for faulty windscreen wipers?

A Easily. You can see they are faulty if they have rubber strips peeling off, if they leave smears on the screen, or if they don't clear the water off properly.

Q How often should I replace the blades?

A About every 12,000 miles or every year is a good rule of thumb. But the real answer is to change them whenever you are not satisfied you can get a good, clear screen.

Q How can I tell if the liquid in my screen-washer is getting low?

A This needs to be checked every day that you drive, before you go out.

Q What happens if I am going on a long journey and the weather is bad?

A Take a spare container in the boot filled with proprietary windscreen-cleaning fluid.

Q What should I do if I am driving on a motorway and my screen-washer dries up?

A You must get off at the next opportunity and replenish it.

Q What happens if my windscreen freezes over and I can't get my screen-washer fluid to work?

A You ought to use a proprietary fluid which does not freeze. But do not use anti-freeze liquid as this will strip the paintwork on the car.

Q How can I tell if my exhaust is legal?

A All MOT garages are now fitted with exhaust-gas analysers. They are quite easy to operate and if you have any doubts get your local garage to check it out, and to show you how they do it too. It is quite interesting and shows you want to play your part in keeping the environment clean.

Q Is the exhaust level for all cars the same?

A No. The newer the car is, the cleaner the exhaust is expected to be. Older cars might not be as efficient and this is allowed for in the MOT exhaust emissions test.

Q   Why should I replace a noisy exhaust silencer?

A   It is more efficient, and makes a lot less noise. Noisy or holed silencers can be dangerous too.

Q   How do I test my seat-belts to see if they work?

A   Sit in your seat with the belt on and jerk forward quickly. The belt should lock up.

Q   How do inertia-reel seat-belts work?

A   They have a locking mechanism built in, rather like a large ball-bearing in a saucer. If the saucer is tilted the ball-bearing moves to one side and locks the belt.

Q   Can I still wear my seat-belts after they have been used in an accident?

A   No. Seat-belts stretch to absorb the energy of stopping. Once they have been stretched they have lost their purpose. Get them replaced.

11. L plates must be properly used and displayed

Proper L plates must be displayed every time a learner driver is behind the wheel or riding a motor cycle, scooter, or moped. They must be visible to the front and rear of the vehicle and readily seen at a reasonable distance. The shape and size of an L plate is quite precise. It has to be a white 18 centimetres (7 inch) square, with a red **L** 10 centimetres (4 inches) high, 9 centimetres (3½ inches) across the base, and 4 centimetres (1½ inches) thick. Although the corners of the white square may be rounded off, it must be flat and upright, not wrapped around bike fork. Except for driving-school cars and when learners are driving they should be removed when a fully licensed driver or rider is driving.

Green L plates and blue P plates are sometimes used by those who are a little bit nervous when they are on their own at first. However they have no validity and are not necessary. Like proper L plates, it is an offence to display anything in the front or back windows of vehicles, as this causes an obstruction to the driver's visibility.

12. The laws regarding learner driver supervision

The duties and qualifications of a supervisor are clear and precise. The supervisor must be at least twenty-one years of age and have held a full licence for that category of vehicle for at least three years. A supervisor must be able to take control of the vehicle at any time, and in the event of any incident happening whilst the learner is driving the supervisor can be found guilty of aiding and abetting any offence committed by the driver. In the case of Approved Driving Instructors, who are the only people allowed by law to teach driving for money or money's worth, any penalty points given as a result of offences committed by a learner driver are even more harsh. ADIs can be removed from the Government's ADI Register if they are given six driving licence penalty points, even though the normal limit for being banned from driving is twelve penalty points.

Although supervision by family or friends is allowed, and in some cases can be very beneficial, it is essential that the insurance cover for the driver, the vehicle, and the fact that driving practice is being given is confirmed by the vehicle insurers and vehicle owners.

FACT FILE

Learner drivers are liable to the same laws as any other motorist or motor cyclist and need to take proper care.

Learner drivers who are not covered by proper third-party insurance can render themselves liable to enormous civil compensation claims if they cause an accident. This is apart from any legal penalties for causing death, injury, or damage as well.

Supervisors of learner drivers must be in a position to actively supervise. It is not enough to accompany them.

Supervising drivers are liable to the same fines and penalties as the drivers they are with.

The best way to supervise learner drivers is to find out from their instructors what they have done, and what they need to practise between their professional lessons.

Q Who is allowed to supervise a learner driver?

A Any full licence holder who is over the age of twenty-one and has held a licence for that category of vehicle for more than three years.

Q Do I need to have dual controls fitted to the car?

A No. But the supervisor must be able to reach the controls if necessary to take over.

Q Is it necessary to fit a second mirror for the supervisor to use?

A It is not a legal requirement, but if the supervisor does not have a mirror it could make life difficult both in an awkward situation and if the incident goes to court.

Q What is the best use I can make of my family offering to sit with me?

A Get them to give you silent practice. You will have learned how to drive with your instructor. Your instructor will give you further things to learn, but you can practise what you already know and can do with your family.

A Are there any legal restrictions on learning to drive in my family car?

A Yes, the legal restrictions are mainly insurance ones. Insurance companies need to know who is driving the vehicle, and for what purpose. They will often charge an additional premium if someone under the age of twenty-five, especially an L driver, is going to drive it. Check it first.

Q What insurance cover must I have when I am being taught in my own or the family car?

A You must have written confirmation from the car's insurers that you are a named driver and allowed to drive although you still need L plates.

13. The laws regarding seat-belt wearing

It is the driver's responsibility to wear a seat-belt all the time they are driving except when they are reversing, or carrying out an exercise which involves a reversing movement. Drivers are also responsible that all children under fourteen years of age are properly belted up if there are seat-belts for them. Passengers over this age must accept liability for wearing their own seat-belts if they are fitted. Children below the age of three must use appropriate child restraints in the front seats, and if they are available wear them in the back seats too. Children may use booster seats, child restraints, or harnesses or proper child seats, but they must be properly fitted.

FACT FILE

Although the age of fourteen is quoted for children to be legally responsible for wearing their own belts as passengers, the law allows the height to be a material factor in whether children should wear adult belts or use booster seats and cushions. If they are under 1.5 metres (5 feet) in height they should use an appropriate child restraint if one is fitted, but they can use an adult seat-belt provided it fits properly. Children aged twelve and thirteen who are over 1.5 metres should use adult belts where fitted.

Q   Who decides what to do if there are more children being carried than there are seat-belts?

A   You, the driver, must choose which children wear the seat-belts available and which don't.

Q   Which children ought to wear the lap and diagonal belts and which the lap belts only?

A   Larger children should be belted up with lap and diagonal belts. Younger children should wear lap belts only if these are all that are left.

Q   Can I sit children in the back of an estate car?

A   Only if there are proper manufacturer's seats and seat-belts for them.

Q   How do child-proof locks work on back doors of cars?

A   They can only be opened from the outside of the car, making it safer to carry young children in the back.

Q   What should I do if a passenger refuses to wear a seat-belt?

A   If they are under fourteen they must do as you tell them. You can refuse to carry those who are older unless they belt up. As a driver it is your responsibility to ensure the occupants are as safe as possible.

Q   Isn't it safer not wearing seat-belts in the event of a fire or danger from drowning?

A If you are wearing a seat-belt when a crash occurs you are more likely to still be conscious to deal with getting out of the belts and the car than if you weren't wearing them.

14. Practical driving skills

The controls of the car are best learned whilst you are sitting in the car on your first practical driving lesson, but it helps to know beforehand what sort of controls there are and how they are used.

You must know and be able to state the use and functions of all the vehicle's controls. They are divided into main controls, that is those which are used directly to control the car, and secondary controls, which include all the gauges, displays, and vehicle warning lights, mostly on the panel in front of the driver. If you are in a driving-school car make sure you get to know each of them, what they mean, how they work and when you need to use them. If you own or drive your own car you will probably need to do this yourself, and you can use the handbook to guide you through them. Certainly the worst time to discover the meaning of a warning light is when it comes on whilst driving late at night, in the rain, on a lonely country road or motorway.

In each case you need to know what each of the controls does, how it does it, and ideally what sort of words are used by your instructor when you are driving.

What it does	How it does it	Words used

Accelerator

Controls the engine speed, but also allows tick-over	Regulates the flow of fuel to the engine	*More, less,* or *off, gas*

Footbrake

Controls the wheel speed	Applies friction to all four wheels	*Cover, brake gently, brake gently to stop*

Clutch

Joins the engine through the gears to the wheels	Connects and separates the engine from the gear box	*Cover clutch, clutch down, **slowly** clutch up.*

Steering-wheel

Enables the car to change direction	Turns the front wheels to the left or right	*Steer* for small moves, *turn the wheel* for right and left turnings

Handbrake (or parking brake – some are operated by foot!)

Locks the rear wheels	Pads and shoes expand to lock brakes	*Apply, prepare or release the handbrake*

Gear lever

Select the gear from a choice of 4, 5, or 6 + Reverse	Enables engine speed to be used efficiently	*Hand on the gear lever, palm towards me or you*

All windows, and especially the front windscreen, must always be kept clean and clear. This is not only with the use of wipers and washers, but by using the heater and demister controls as well. Windscreens must also be free from cracks or other damage which can impair your vision. Whilst tinted screens are not necessarily illegal, they can certainly impair your vision. If you cannot read a number plate at the required distance through one you could be breaking the law.

For the first time you need to spend quite a time setting up your mirrors, especially the door mirrors. Apart from the need to see through them clearly, the fact you have adjusted them will act as a prompt to use them more. Most drivers fail to use their door mirrors enough, especially the passenger door mirror.

Q Why doesn't the car stop when the accelerator pedal is not pressed?

A The engine has a tick-over control which stops the car from stalling when no acceleration is needed. This also enables you to approach corners and junctions with the brake and clutch covered without stalling.

Q How does the choke work?

A The choke limits the amount of air mixing with the petrol to produce a richer gas–air mixture to make it easier to start the car and run it when it is cold.

Q How soon after starting should I put the choke back in?

A After two or three minutes is normal.

Q What happens if I drive for a long distance with the choke out?

A This means you are getting too much unburned petrol flowing into the cylinders, and this will dilute the oil which will eventually cause damage.

Q Are all cars fitted with choke controls?

A No; most new cars are fitted with fuel injection and catalytic converters. These don't need chokes because their fuel mixture is calculated automatically. Other cars have automatic chokes which save you worrying. Some cars use diesel fuel and this has a different ignition system entirely.

Q What is a catalytic converter?

A This is means of making the fuel system more ecologically pure. It helps to get rid of harmful exhaust emissions by filtering them out.

Q Does this make an engine more efficient?

A   Not really, in fact the performance drops, but it does make for a cleaner environment.

Q   Is this why most new cars use unleaded fuel?

A   Yes. Unleaded fuel gives a cleaner exhaust, but leaded fuel can damage engines and catalytic converters, so care must be taken not to use the wrong fuel.

Q   Is there any way I can tell if I am about to put four-star leaded fuel into an unleaded tank?

A   Yes, the leaded fuel nozzle will not fit into the tank because unleaded fuel tanks have smaller entrances to remind you.

Q   Does it do any harm to put unleaded fuel into an older engine that needs leaded fuel?

A   Not initially, though you will notice some misfiring; but if you use it a lot it can cause a great deal of damage.

Q   Are there any extra things I should remember about cars fitted with catalysers?

A   Yes. You must never try to push start them, or drive them if the engine misfires.

Q   Why should I not drive a catalytic fitted car when it misfires?

A   Because unburned petrol going through the converter will damage and destroy the catalytic elements.

Q   Are there any other things I need to be careful about when driving a car fitted with a catalyser?

A   Yes, you need to avoid making too many short journeys from a cold start. And avoid driving over road humps at speed. The honeycomb filter inside the catalyser is made from ceramics which are very brittle when cold.

Q   How should I brake in normal stopping?

A   Progressively.

Q   What is meant by progressive braking?

A   Another description is tapered braking. You brake gently at first to take up the feel of the tyres gripping the road surface. Then you brake harder to get maximum benefit from the brakes, then as you slow down you gently taper the braking effort off until you can scarcely feel the change of speed as you stop.

Q   How can I practise this form of tapered stopping?

A   Practise pulling the car up to rest at designated places so that the final stop causes no jerk or snatch.

Q   What is an emergency stop?

A   Stopping in an emergency means bring the car to rest as quickly as you can but with safety. There are two things to bear in mind.

If you are in danger of hitting something you really do have to hit the brakes hard, but you must avoid skidding or locking the front wheels.

Q   How can I practise stopping in an emergency?

A   Ideally get the feel of the brakes and what is needed whilst stationary. Then practise getting from the accelerator pedal to the brake at slow speeds, and practise at higher speeds until you are proficient, quick, and safe up to 30 mph.

Q   What does it mean if they say the brakes are spongy?

A   Spongy brakes means that air or water has got into the brake-fluid lines. When the fluid gets hot, if it is contaminated in any way, the water in the system turns to steam and is easily compressed. This reduces the effectiveness of the brakes as pure brake fluid cannot be compressed. Have your brakes checked regularly and the fluid replaced about every three years.

Q   Should I use my mirrors before I use my brakes in an emergency?

A   No, but you should always know what is behind you, and as soon as you have braked hard you should have time to check your mirrors anyway.

Q   Isn't there any danger from being hit from behind when you brake suddenly?

A   Yes, this is why you must always know what is behind you. Then you know whether you can brake safely or not.

Q   Should I use the handbrake to assist stopping?

A   No, only apply the handbrake when you have actually stopped. Its use is only as a parking brake.

Q   What is wrong with resting my foot on the clutch pedal whilst I am driving?

A   This puts pressure on the thrust bearing and can easily wear it out. Keep your left foot away from the clutch.

Q   Are there any other dangers with resting my left foot near to the pedal but without pushing it down?

A   Yes, because it tempts you to put your clutch down too soon in an emergency.

Q   Why is it wrong to de-clutch in an emergency?

A   There are occasions when you should put it down, but if you do it without thinking it can easily cause front-wheel lock-up on front-wheel-drive cars. This can cause the very skids you are trying to avoid.

Q   Why is skidding wrong?

A Skidding is illegal; but it means you are out of control and will hit whatever is in front of you.

Q How should you stop in an emergency?

A If you know you won't be hit from behind hit the foot brake firmly, then increase the pressure as hard as you can. The intention is to stop as quickly and safely as possible. If you do feel that the brakes are about to lock up, ease off the pressure, allow the weight to come back off the front and then brake again.

Q What is cadence braking?

A Cadence braking is this type of braking (sometimes called weight transfer or rhythm braking) which enables you to steer whilst you are not braking and to slow down whilst you are. Each time the brake is pumped hard the brakes are most effective at a point just before the brakes lock. As you get slower you can continue to brake for longer as the lock-up point is later.

Q What is pulse braking?

A This is a variation on cadence braking, but you brake on and off in a steady rhythm trying to keep the weight of the car relatively even so that the braking effect of all four wheels is maximized.

Q Does ABS braking help?

A Yes, but all ABS does is to allow you to steer and brake together without locking up the driving wheels.

Q Does that mean that ABS allows you to stop more quickly?

A No. ABS cannot stop you any quicker than a car without ABS.

Q What position should my hands be on when I am steering?

A Both hands should be on the wheel at the ten-to-two position, or slightly lower on the nine-to-three.

Q Why is it wrong to hold the wheel with one hand, or much lower down?

A Because when you want to steer quickly your hands are not free enough.

Q Is it wrong to cross your hands on the steering-wheel?

A No, but you must not allow your hands to become locked onto the wheel, which they can if you cross them unnecessarily.

Q When can you cross your hands on the steering-wheel, then?

A You may cross them if it helps you during slow speed man-oeuvres; but you still need to avoid getting them locked up or unable to turn the wheel back again.

Q Is it allowed to miss out gears when losing speed?

A Yes. The normal rule is that you brake once, and change gear once, for every hazard that you slow down for.

Q   Does that mean you must always block change through the gears?

A   No, you must think each gear change through, and select the one that you will need next.

Q   How about going faster and up through the gears – can you miss out gears then?

A   There are occasions when you can miss out a gear going up. The most obvious time is when you are in second gear at about 10 mph, increasing it quickly to 28 mph and then keeping your speed down at the built-up area speed limit. You can miss out third gear if you need second gear to accelerate hard.

Q   How often would you miss out gears going up?

A   Not very often; you would normally build up your speed and change progressively.

Q   Is it possible to use fifth gear in town driving?

A   Yes, it is normally possible, but it depends on how much load you are putting on the engine and gears. If you are trying to pick up speed or go up a hill then a lower gear would be more suitable, even at 28–30 mph.

15. What are a driver's responsibilities to all other road users?

The driver's responsibilities are always total. Driving is not a right, but a privilege. At all times the driver must assume that someone else may take priority, especially where the law reinforces that priority. But some road users, especially the very young, the elderly, and the infirm, are not always capable of making reasoned and reasonable judgements, therefore the driver is always obliged to give way gracefully where necessary.

16. A supervisor's responsibilities

When supervising a new or young driver the supervising driver must not only accept full responsibility for what the driver does, the supervisor must also take on the responsibility for advising and guiding the learner driver. This is why the responsibility of an

Approved Driving Instructor is so great. In fact if an Approved Driving Instructor gives wrong advice or allows a learner to absorb bad habits he or she can be removed from the Government register and lose what employment they may have had.

FACT FILE

The responsibility, both of the driver and any supervisor, is not just to other road users generally, it covers such things as proper and safe vehicle loading and passenger loading.

Vehicles must not have improper or unsafe loads, nor must there be more passengers than there are seats. The only exception to this is when very young children are carried. Three or four young children may be seated in the back of a car even though there may only be proper seats and seat-belts for two or three. However it is the driver's and supervisor's responsibilities to ensure that each child is properly seated, and as many as are able are belted or secured in.

Q   How important is it that learner drivers are responsible in law even on their first driving lesson?

A   It is very important for learner drivers to realize that they are bound by the same rules and regulations as fully licensed drivers. This is why a good background theoretical knowledge is important even before they sit behind the wheel for the first time.

Q   What is the extent of a driver's responsibility with regard to the motor car?

A   Drivers must know that they are legally licensed and entitled to drive, that the vehicle they are in is taxed with the tax disc displayed, and that they, the vehicle they are in, and the purpose for which it is being used are fully covered for insurance against any third-party claim.

Q   Are there any other responsibilities?

A   Drivers must observe the principles laid down in the Highway Code at all times, and do all that they can to avoid breaking any laws, Highway Code rules, or traffic regulations. They must also drive with due care and consideration for all other road users at all times.

Q   What penalties can be imposed on a driver who does not abide by these rules and regulations?

A   Drivers found guilty of any traffic offence can be fined, given penalty points, or sent to prison. Drivers guilty of serious driving offences, or building up a total of twelve or more penalty points in any three years, can be banned from driving.

Q   Are any offences considered serious enough to cause an immediate ban?

A   Some offences of very bad driving, such as those involving racing, or drink driving, carry an automatic disqualification penalty. Magistrates and judges are also allowed to cause drivers to take their driving test, or possibly an extended driving test, before being allowed back on the road again.

Q   What is an extended driving test?

A   Drivers found guilty of very bad driving offences can be caused to take an extended driving test. This lasts twice as long as the normal test (seventy minutes instead of thirty-five minutes' driving) and covers about twenty-two miles.

Q   Do these drivers need to take another theory test as well?

A   Yes, banned drivers who must take another driving test must pass the theoretical written examination for that category of vehicle as well as the practical test.

17. Safety checks when entering a vehicle

When first entering a car the driver must ensure that it is safe to drive, and that they carry out proper safety precautions before moving off. The safety checks should be carried out each time the vehicle is re-entered. If you are the only driver and you use the vehicle regularly some checks need only be cursory ones. If it is a driving-school vehicle, or you only have use of it occasionally or for driving lessons, you need to be very careful, precise, and positive in the way you carry out the checks.

FACT FILE

The entry sequence is as follows:

Look all round the vehicle before you get in. Look at the tyres and windscreens and also look for objects which may be behind or in front of the wheels.

Check that it is safe to do so before opening any door.

Get in and close the driver's door quickly but safely and properly.

Feel and shake the door to make sure it is properly closed.

Check all other doors are closed too, and that the handbrake or parking brake is properly applied.

Then check and adjust as necessary the position of your seat.

Remember that some seats move up and down, and you can adjust the backrest rake as well as back and forward.

Can you reach the steering-wheel and all the controls properly and safely?

Put on your seat-belt, lock it up firmly, make sure it is comfortable, and see that everyone else in the car is properly belted in too.

Then adjust the mirrors for maximum view all round. And consciously tell yourself where all the blind spots are.

Q   Why do you need to walk all round the car before you get in?

A   You never know what or who may have crept up behind whilst the car has been left alone. It is not just cats and hedgehogs who may creep up for warmth. Many tiny children have been killed because the driver didn't know they were there.

Q   Where do you check before opening the door to get in?

A   Look for cars and other vehicles, including cyclists, who may be coming on you whilst you are getting in. It is even more important to do this when it is raining or windy.

Q How can you tell your car door is properly closed?

A Car doors have a double lock; if you don't give it that extra pull it might be only on the first catch still.

Q What happens if you don't check the door?

A Have you ever seen a car move off and a door swing open suddenly and dangerously? Don't let it happen to you.

Q Why should you check the parking brake immediately you get into the car?

A If the handbrake has not been set, getting in could suddenly allow the car to roll forward. If it has been left in gear and you put your clutch down it will certainly move.

Q Why do you adjust your seat before putting on the seat-belt?

A Have you ever tried to adjust your seat when wearing a seat-belt? It is quite difficult.

Q How should you adjust your centre mirror?

A So that you can see as much as possible through the rear window.

18. Having entered safely the cockpit drill follows before starting the engine

This sequence must be followed every time you start or restart the engine. Remember that you also have to do if you stall.

The rules are simple: always check that the handbrake is properly applied and then make sure that the gear lever is in neutral. Only then can you turn the key to start the engine.

Q Why do you always need to check before starting the engine?

A If you don't you could be in gear and switching on the starter motor will jerk you forward out of control.

Q Does it matter what sequence you check?

A Yes, if you checked the gear lever and moved it out of gear into neutral and your handbrake wasn't properly on you could roll.

Q But aren't you supposed to check the handbrake when you first get into the car?

A Yes, of course, but that was an initial check. This is to make sure your car is stopped safely and properly parked, before you put it into neutral every time you start the engine. You may have to do this ten or fifteen times during a normal day's driving.

Q   Do you have to carry out this manoeuvre even when you have stalled in traffic and need to get away quickly?

A   This is the proper sequence, and if you have time you should follow it.

Q   What if you really need to get away immediately?

A   If you are sure that you are in first gear, and your clutch is down, it is acceptable to start with the clutch down instead of neutral. But if you are in another gear by mistake you'll probably stall when you move off instead.

19. Safety checks when leaving the vehicle

Always apply the handbrake firmly. Then make sure the gear lever is in neutral, switch off the engine, and remove the key.

   Then when you get out make sure you have put any valuable items out of sight or removed from the car. When you lock the doors always use the key. And then keep the key safe.

FACT FILE

Always switch off your headlights before leaving.

Always leave the handbrake properly set.

Leave the car in neutral unless you are parking on a steep hill.

Only leave it in gear if it is really necessary.

If you leave it in gear make sure you remember when you get back in

---

Q   Why do you need to lock the door with a key?

A   If you use the key you won't lock it in the car.

Q   Why should you not normally leave the car in gear?

A   Because if someone gets in and doesn't check the car could start in gear.

Q   What is the danger of starting in gear?

A   You can easily kill a child or bump another car if you start in gear.

Q   Should you leave parking lights on at night when you leave?

A   You can do, but you only need to if the street lighting is not good.
Q   Where should you park your vehicle?
A   Always park in the safest and most convenient place. Think seriously about not obstructing any other road users or house-holders when you park.

20. Head restraints

Some drivers don't like their head restraints in their cars, and take them out. This is stupid. Head restraints are designed for a purpose. They can save neck injuries and these are the most common ones that drivers suffer in minor bumps, especially when they hit from behind.

21. The procedures of driving

Before you start learning to drive you need to know one or two basic rules of procedures when driving. These are quite simple. When driving straight ahead you need to keep close to the pavement – about 1 metre (3 feet) from it – and a good safe distance from what is ahead.

The safety procedures to be followed when moving off are easy: only move off when you can safely join the stream of traffic.

Similar rules apply to steering and stopping.

FACT FILE

The basic procedure always to be applied throughout your driving career is

| **MIRROR** | **SIGNAL** | **MANOEUVRE** |

Followed by

| **POSITION** | **SPEED** | **LOOK** |

Look can be divided into

| **LOOK** | **ASSESS** | **DECIDE** |

Check your mirrors before you make any decision to change your position or speed.

Make sure you signal your intentions by in-dicators or by arm to anyone who might

---

benefit from knowing what your intentions are.

Then adjust your position and/or your speed; you adjust your speed by braking, accelerating, or decelerating.

As you begin to arrive at junctions or any other hazards continue looking all round, especially to the sides at junctions, then assess what the options are before choosing the safest decision to make.

The Learner Driver Theory Test Paper 1

Thirty-five Questions on the Theoretical Training Syllabus for Learner Drivers

> **Choose the answers nearest to the options given which you think are correct; check your score against the answers shown on the answer page and then work out your score. The minimum acceptable score is 26 but before you consider yourself really ready to take the practical driving test you should score at least 32 out of 35.**
>
> **Where more than one answer is needed, all must be correct to count.**
>
> **Marks scored** **/35**

Allow forty minutes for this test. Answer without using any books or assistance.

1   When driving down a quiet residential street you hear musical chimes and then see an ice-cream van parked on your side of the road 100 metres (109 yards) ahead. There are a number of parked cars on both sides of the road, but no room for oncoming traffic to pass you and the ice-cream van. Which TWO of the following should you do?

A   Move out the centre of the road and maintain your speed.
B   Look out for children emerging from behind parked cars and vans.
C   Use your mirrors, slow down, and be prepared to stop.
D   Pull in and stop at the kerbside until the ice-cream van has gone.

A ( )   B ( )   C ( )   D ( )

2   You are driving along a single-carriageway road at 30 mph in a built-up area. You are conscious that the vehicle behind, occupied by two young men, is getting very close to you. There is no room to overtake, but the driver behind is continually flashing his lights at you. What should you do?
A   Maintain your speed and concentrate on driving safely.
B   Pick up speed and try to get away from him.
C   Slow down and hope that the driver will get past you soon.
D   Attract the attention of the first police officer you see by sounding your horn.

A ( )   B ( )   C ( )   D ( )

3   The effect of a front-wheel blow-out on the nearside will be felt by the driver by which sensation?
A   A slight pull to the right.
B   A strong pull to the left.
C   The rear end starting to snake.
D   The car swinging violently to the left and right.

A ( )   B ( )   C ( )   D ( )

4   All motor cars first registered more than three years ago are required to pass an MOT vehicle inspection. Which of the following would *not* cause failure of this test?
A   A defective exhaust system.
B   Steering-wheel play of half an inch.
C   A defective fog-light.
D   An empty screen-washer bottle.

A ( )   B ( )   C ( )   D ( )

5 What is the minimum total stopping distance for a motor car travelling at 20 mph on a dry road in good conditions?
A   10 metres (32 feet).
B   12 metres (39 feet).
C   15 metres (49 feet).
D   18 metres (59 feet).

A ( )   B ( )   C ( )   D ( )

6 During a short sharp shower of light rain after a long dry spell, all drivers are advised that they must take particular care. Which of the following would be a driver's immediate concern?
A   The condition of the windscreen glass and wipers.
B   Skidding on very greasy road conditions.
C   Cleaning the headlight and rear light lenses.
D   Avoiding dazzling oncoming traffic with the headlights.

A ( )   B ( )   C ( )   D ( )

7 What is the minimum amount of alcohol which would be likely to have an effect on the driving performance of a female driver, about 8 stone in weight?
A   One glass of white wine.
B   Three glasses of white wine.
C   Two pints of lager.
D   A single measure of rum or whisky.

A ( )   B ( )   C ( )   D ( )

8 If you are driving on a long journey at night, which of the following would be most helpful for you to stay awake and alert?
A   Driving with the side windows open.
B   Keeping the radio on full power with loud music.
C   Stopping at intervals for a short walk around the car.
D   Talking to yourself.

A ( )   B ( )   C ( )   D ( )

9   Which set of two age groups of pedestrians is most vulnerable to road-traffic accidents involving vehicles and themselves?
A   5–10 year olds and those over 65.
B   12–17 year olds and those over 60.
C   21–25 year olds and 45–55 year olds.
D   30–35 year olds and those over 70.

A ( )   B ( )   C ( )   D ( )

10   Young drivers consist of about 10% of the total driving population. What percentage of serious road-traffic accidents involve drivers in this age group?
A   5%
B   10%
C   20%
D   30%

A ( )   B ( )   C ( )   D ( )

11   You are following a large heavy goods vehicle through a busy town. It indicates that it intends to turn left, then immediately swings out to the right. What should you do?
A   Overtake on the inside as it is obviously intending to turn right.
B   Overtake on the right, as it is signalling left.
C   Drop back and wait before making any decision.
D   Sound your horn to attract the driver's attention to his error.

A ( )   B ( )   C ( )   D ( )

12   At a narrow crossroads in town you wish to turn right. Facing you is a large bus, which is also signalling to turn right. Which of the following is the safest procedure to follow?
A   Stop where you are and wait for the bus to complete its turn.
B   Move off quickly and turn before the bus starts to move forward.
C   Move forward slowly, making eye contact with the bus driver.
D   Wave to the bus driver, telling them to cross first.

A ( )   B ( )   C ( )   D ( )

13   You are driving on a single-carriageway road in a queue of traffic all driving at about 30 mph; ahead of you is some oncoming

traffic. You realize you are being overtaken by a large car which goes past you and you feel that it will try to cut in. What do you do?

A　Close the gap between you and the vehicle ahead.
B　Drop back immediately and create a larger gap.
C　Sound your horn to warn the driver not to cut in.
D　Maintain your speed and flash your headlights.

A ( )　　B ( )　　C ( )　　D ( )

14　You are waiting to turn right across a busy single carriageway into a railway-station entrance. A motor cyclist is waiting to turn right out of the same entrance. Both of you are prevented from moving by the constant stream of traffic coming towards you. There is a slight gap in the traffic and the leading vehicle flashes its lights at you. What should you do?

A　Wait until the driver obviously slows down before crossing.
B　Cross immediately into the station entrance, keeping eye contact.
C　Wait for the motor cyclist to emerge first, then cross if there is time.
D　Flash your lights to thank the driver and then cross quickly.

A ( )　　B ( )　　C ( )　　D ( )

15　You are driving along in a 40 mph speed limit on a busy dual carriageway with gaps for right turns at intervals. The left lane is full of slow-moving trucks and cars. You are in the right-hand lane but ahead of you is a motor car bearing a P plate only travelling at 25 mph. You wish to continue ahead, what should you do?

A　Flash your lights to attract the driver's attention.
B　Overtake this vehicle on the left lane.
C　Slow down and wait to see if the vehicle is turning right.
D　Close the gap so that the driver ahead is more aware of you.

A ( )　　B ( )　　C ( )　　D ( )

16　Two children are waiting on the pavement alongside an uncontrolled zebra crossing. No one else is on the crossing and they appear to be waiting to cross. You are the first vehicle in a queue of traffic and you are travelling at 20 mph about 15 metres (49 feet) from the crossing. What should you do?

A   Stop quickly and wave the children to cross the road.

B   Check your mirrors, give an arm signal, and slow down to stop.

C   Speed up to get through the crossing before the children step on it.

D   Stop your car and wave other traffic down to allow precedence.

A ( )   B ( )   C ( )   D ( )

17   You are driving along a busy road in town following a bus whose passengers stand up and start moving towards the door at the back. The bus stops and you find you are too close to move out to pass it. Other traffic drives past you and then it is clear behind. What should you do?

A   Reverse slightly and check to see if it is clear to pass it.

B   Reverse quickly and get past the bus quickly.

C   Wait where you are until the bus eventually moves off.

D   Sound your horn to remind the bus driver of your presence.

A ( )   B ( )   C ( )   D ( )

18   You are driving on a dual carriageway at 60 mph following a large goods vehicle with a loaded trailer. It is raining heavily and there is a lot of surface water and spray from vehicles. You pull out to see if it is safe to overtake; no one is following you and the overtaking lane seems clear. Which TWO of the following do you do?

A   Drop down a gear before accelerating gently past the LGV.

B   Flash your lights as you drive past the LGV.

C   Use your washers to keep the windscreen clear whilst alongside.

D   Check your mirrors when you are past before getting back in.

A ( )   B ( )   C ( )   D ( )

19   You are driving at 15 mph along a residential area which has been pedestrianized in some places. Traffic calming measures are being used; these consist of sleeping policemen about 25 centimetres (6 inches) high across the road. What is the best way to drive over these bumps?

A   Quickly to allow the suspension to settle.
B   Sounding your horn as you drive over each one.
C   Declutching as your wheels go over each of the bumps.
D   Steering at an angle so each wheel is lifted in turn.

A ( )   B ( )   C ( )   D ( )

20 You are driving in a city suburb at night time well illuminated by good sodium street lights. What lights would you use on your own vehicle?
A   Side and rear lights only.
B   Headlights on dipped beam.
C   Headlights on main beam.
D   Low-slung front driving lights.

A ( )   B ( )   C ( )   D ( )

21 What is the speed limit for a new driver who is driving on a rural motorway for the first time?
A   50 mph.
B   60 mph.
C   70 mph.
D   No limit.

A ( )   B ( )   C ( )   D ( )

22 When driving along a motorway the normal lane to be in is the left-hand lane (lane one). Under which TWO of the following circumstances would it be suitable to drive in the middle lane (lane two)?
A   When there is no other traffic on the motorway within half a mile.
B   When other traffic may be joining from an acceleration lane.
C   When overtaking a slower-moving vehicle in lane three.
D   When overtaking slower-moving traffic in lane one.

A ( )   B ( )   C ( )   D ( )

23 The national speed limit for a single-carriageway road is
A   50 mph.
B   55 mph.
C   60 mph.
D   70 mph.

A ( )   B ( )   C ( )   D ( )

24   A driver in a strange area can always tell what the speed limit is by looking for signs and indications. Which TWO of the following are clues to the speed limit in force for any particular road?
A   All towns have a maximum speed limit of 30 mph on all roads.
B   Built-up areas have a 30 mph limit unless signed differently.
C   Street lighting less than 200 metres (218 yards) apart signifies a built-up area.
D   All road have a speed limit of 70 mph unless signed differently.

A ( )   B ( )   C ( )   D ( )

25   Shapes and colours are used to indicate different types of road sign. A blue circle generally indicates which of the following?
A   Warning sign.
B   Prohibitory sign.
C   Mandatory sign.
D   Information sign.

A ( )   B ( )   C ( )   D ( )

26   Shapes and colours are used to indicate different types of road sign. A green rectangle generally indicates which of the following?
A   Motorway sign.
B   Prohibitory sign.
C   Mandatory sign.
D   Information sign.

A ( )   B ( )   C ( )   D ( )

27   You are stopped whilst driving a five-year-old vehicle and asked by a police officer to produce the documents which apply to you driving that vehicle. Which list of documents would you be required to produce?
A   Driving licence, vehicle insurance, and tax disc.
B   Driving licence, vehicle insurance, and MOT test certificate.
C   Driving licence and vehicle registration document.
D   Vehicle insurance and MOT test certificate.

A ( )   B ( )   C ( )   D ( )

28   You are driving a vehicle which has no MOT certificate in force

and you are stopped by a police officer. Which two of the following reasons are valid and acceptable?

A   You are on your way to a pre-booked MOT test appointment.
B   Your vehicle has failed its MOT test and you are taking it home.
C   The vehicle was only first registered 3½ years ago.
D   The MOT certificate has expired by less than 14 days.

A ( )   B ( )   C ( )   D ( )

29   You are the first to arrive at the scene of an accident. There are no serious injuries but the vehicles involved cannot readily be removed from the scene. Which of the following should you consider first?

A   Help the less seriously injured get out of their vehicles.
B   Give drinks and cigarettes to any who need them.
C   Switch off engines and impose a smoking ban.
D   Run to the nearest phone box to get help.

A ( )   B ( )   C ( )   D ( )

30   You have a breakdown and your vehicle may cause an obstruction. At what distance from the vehicle should you place a red warning triangle?

A   10 metres (32 feet).
B   15 metres (49 feet).
C   25 metres (89 feet).
D   50 metres (164 feet).

A ( )   B ( )   C ( )   D ( )

31   The vehicle you are in is being towed by another. What is the maximum length of tow rope which may be used?

A   2.5 metres (8 feet).
B   3 metres (10 feet).
C   4 metres (13 feet).
D   4.5 metres (15 feet).

A ( )   B ( )   C ( )   D ( )

32   You are driving your motor car which has five seats including that for the driver. You are asked to carry six people including two young children and yourself. Which of the following is correct?

A   One child must sit on an adult's lap in the front seat.
B   Both children must be carried in the rear seats.
C   There must be enough seats for all passengers.
D   Seat belts need not be worn in the rear seats.

A ( )   B ( )   C ( )   D ( )

33 You are driving in a busy town with lots of cyclists and pedestrians. You intend to turn left at the next road ahead, but there are cyclists on your left. What should you do?
A   Overtake the cyclists quickly so that they can see your left signal.
B   Wait for the cyclists to get past you before signalling left.
C   Sound your horn to make them aware you are turning.
D   Keep close to the left-hand kerb to avoid them coming inside you.

A ( )   B ( )   C ( )   D ( )

34   What is the purpose of the yellow zigzag lines often found along the kerbside on some roads in residential areas?
A   School entrance – keep clear.
B   Pedestrian crossing ahead.
C   Waiting restricted at any time.
D   Loading restricted during day time.

A ( )   B ( )   C ( )   D ( )

35   You are driving in the middle lane, lane two, of a rural motorway in a busy stream of traffic. Ahead you can see vehicles applying their hazard warning lights in all three lanes. What should you do?
A   Wait until you see warning signs on the central reservation.
B   Get into the left lane, lane one, as quickly as possible.
C   Use your mirrors, brake gently, and use your own hazard warning lights.
D   Move out into the right-hand lane, lane three, to see better.

A ( )   B ( )   C ( )   D ( )

Show this to your driving instructor so that you may discuss the questions and the answers you have given together. It may be necessary to take more training, or to continue your private studies, before you take another mock theory driving test.

The Learner Driver Theory Test – Answer Sheet Paper 1

1		2		3		4		5	
A	□	A	X	A	□	A	□	A	□
B	X	B	□	B	X	B	X	B	X
C	X	C	□	C	□	C	□	C	□
D	□	D	□	D	□	D	□	D	□

6		7		8		9		10	
A	□	A	X	A	□	A	□	A	□
B	X	B	□	B	□	B	X	B	□
C	□	C	□	C	X	C	□	C	X
D	□	D	□	D	□	D	□	D	□

11		12		13		14		15	
A	□	A	□	A	□	A	X	A	□
B	□	B	□	B	X	B	□	B	□
C	X	C	X	C	□	C	□	C	X
D	□	D	□	D	□	D	□	D	□

16		17		18		19		20	
A	□	A	X	A	X	A	□	A	□
B	X	B	□	B	□	B	□	B	X
C	□	C	□	C	□	C	X	C	□
D	□	D	□	D	X	D	□	D	□

21		22		23		24		25	
A	□	A	□	A	□	A	□	A	□
B	□	B	X	B	□	B	X	B	□
C	X	C	□	C	X	C	X	C	X
D	□	D	X	D	□	D	□	D	□

26		27		28		29		30	
A	□	A	□	A	X	A	□	A	□
B	□	B	X	B	X	B	□	B	□
C	□	C	□	C	□	C	X	C	□
D	X	D	□	D	□	D	□	D	X

31		32		33		34		35	
A	□	A	□	A	□	A	X	A	□
B	□	B	□	B	X	B	□	B	□
C	□	C	X	C	□	C	□	C	X
D	X	D	□	D	□	D	□	D	□

On the Road

Once you have started driving you need to be fully aware of *all* your responsibilities as a driver. Questions will be asked about them.

1. Your responsibilities

As a driver, whether licensed and experienced or an absolute novice taking your driving instructor's car out for your very first on-road lesson, you must realize that you are fully responsible for every action you take. You must listen carefully to what your instructor tells you to do, and to do it to the best of your ability. This is why it is essential that all your early driving lessons are taken with a properly qualified Department of Transport Approved Driving Instructor. Professional instructors are trained to teach and will not put responsibility on to new drivers until they are ready to accept it.

They will not only teach you how to use the controls, which is the easy bit, they will also teach you how to position yourself and your car on the road, and how to take your place safely and confidently in any stream of traffic. They will also teach you the need for constant alertness. Regrettably, it is not possible to pinpoint the cause of accidents and say that people who do certain things should be banned. Accidents are usually caused by an overall lack of care and attention. This is a factor which affects us at all times; every driver suffers from lack of concentration occasionally. It is just that it happens to some drivers much more than others. This is something you can choose to do, right from your first lesson. You can choose to be a caring and careful driver, or you can choose not to bother – and suffer the consequences.

The reason for this lack of concentration on the driving task, and of a proper awareness of what is happening all around, is harder to define. In some cases it is sheer carelessness, in others boredom or lack of interest. The cause is usually bad initial driver training. A good instructor is really needed: your professional driving instructor will pay particular attention to the need for you to be aware of your responsibilities towards others and how to show proper care and consideration towards them.

A professional driving instructor's essential skill is to create within you the desire to become a good, safe driver who will always see the need – and be willing – to concentrate on driving well.

One of the greatest skills your instructor will teach you is how to develop a proper sense of anticipation. Many experienced drivers are careless, but over the years they have developed a sense of self-preservation which enables them – usually – to get out of danger situations with only a few bumps and scratches on their cars. Most drivers seem to have a bump or two every year, but inexperienced drivers have not yet acquired the skills to get them out of trouble. This is why youngsters and new drivers – who consist of less than 10% of the driving population – are involved in more than 22% of serious accidents and road deaths. It is also why young car thieves who steal cars to show off their alleged skills to their chums always come to grief eventually. They know how the accelerator works and they can steer relatively well; they even think they know how to carry out the infamous 'handbrake turn'. It is when the real tests of vehicle handling are needed that their limited range of skills runs dry and they find they cannot control the car after all.

Professional driving instructors are taught to present their lessons in such a way that your interest in driving well has top priority and you will never become bored with driving or allow yourself to become distracted.

FACT FILE

All drivers are responsible for their actions whilst in a motor car.

They must remain alert to the actions of other road users.

They must not be distracted from the driving task.

> **Accidents are mainly caused by lack of at-
> tention or not correctly anticipating a chan-
> ging road and traffic situation.**
>
> **Drivers must show courtesy and considera-
> tion to all other road users, and give priority
> to others – even when it is taken by them
> wrongly.**

Q Is a learner driver considered to be in charge of a vehicle?
A Yes, at all times, although the supervisor must accept joint responsibility.
Q What is the main cause of accidents?
A Driver error, usually made worse by lack of attention to what is about to happen.
Q How can a driver avoid becoming involved in road accidents?
A By concentrating on the driving task at all times.
Q How do I avoid getting bored when I am driving?
A Boredom is another way of saying lack of interest. Get interested in safe driving and you will not become bored.
Q How can driving be made interesting?
A Driving can be interesting at all times if you apply yourself to it properly. Realize you are in charge of a machine which can cause damage if not handled correctly, and be an enormous benefit if used intelligently.
Q Why should learner drivers be held responsible for being safe even on their first lesson?
A Because learning to drive is not just about understanding what the controls of the car do, it is much more concerned with what the driver does with that car.
Q Are there any special rules about sharing the road with other vehicles?
A Yes, remember that driving is a privilege and we can only use that privilege if we are courteous and considerate to all other road users.
Q How about when I am sharing the road with larger vehicles like commercial trucks and coaches?
A Remember that larger vehicles cannot accelerate, brake, or steer as quickly as you can, and make allowances for this.
Q Are there any things I need to remember about driving with large trucks?

A Yes. They are longer and take up more space. They also need more time to join traffic flows and it will take you a longer time to overtake them.

Q Do I need to pay any attention to the mirrors of large trucks and buses?

A Yes, if you cannot see the driver's face in his door mirrors he probably can't see you either.

Q How should I overtake a large truck?

A With care; remember that on a level road it will take an extra five or ten seconds to get past a truck when you overtake.

Q Is it any easier to overtake a truck going downhill?

A No, because the truck can pick up speed more easily it will take you even longer.

Q How can I learn responsibility?

A By listening to what your instructor says, and by doing what you are told.

Q Are there any legal penalties for not being a responsible driver?

A Yes. You can lose your licence to drive, you can be fined up to £5,000 and you can even be sent to prison.

Q Are there any other penalties for bad driving?

A Yes indeed. Apart from your moral responsibilities to safeguard other road users, there is the fact that bad drivers or those who are punished by the law usually have to pay very high insurance premiums.

Q Is safe and responsible driving a matter of habit?

A Yes. Good habits are easy to acquire, especially if you have a good teacher.

Q Why is it best not to learn to drive with a friend or a member of the family?

A There is a danger of learning their bad habits, and bad habits are more difficult to break or change.

Q Why are drivers expected to show care and consideration to other road users when they don't have priority?

A Courtesy is the real clue to road safety. Some people will always barge in and push their way around, some drivers will use their weight to take priority; but it is not just courtesy to avoid confrontations, it is common sense.

Q What happens when two road users both use their weight to take priority?

A This is when really stupid accidents happen, and you must do what you can to avoid them.

Q Should I always give priority to other road users even when they don't expect it?

A No, you should learn the correct sequences of priority, and when it is your turn you should expect to go – in safety. It is only when stupid people, regardless of what vehicles they may be in, bully their way through that you have to accept their bad manners gracefully.

Q How about pedestrians – should I give them priority when they are crossing the road?

A You must never frighten them if they are crossing. But don't invite them to cross in a dangerous place, just because they are waiting to do so.

2. The effects of stress, ageing, and ill health on drivers and other road users

Not all drivers and other road users make mistakes because they deliberately seek confrontations, of course; they make mistakes for a whole series of reasons: not all drivers and bike riders are well taught, horse riders have comparatively very little control over their animals, and children are often not interested in road safety, only in the games they are playing. However one of the greatest problems with other road users is that we are all subject to the results of stress, pressure, and distraction.

Stress affects us all. Sometimes we make mistakes because we feel we must act immediately instead of waiting to decide on the safest course of action. Often we find that the effects of what we are doing at home or at work or school badly affects how we behave with our cars or motor cycles. If something is really worrying you it is better not to drive or ride whilst it affects the way you behave.

Ageing also has a negative effect, but there is no hard and fast rule that says that drivers and full licence holders are safe until they reach the age of – say – seventy (when driving licences have to be renewed) and then suddenly go gaga. Ageing can have peculiar effects on people; one of the most noticeable effects is that you usually become more cautious about things which require skill and dexterity. Age brings with it stiffening of the limbs, which makes it more difficult to perform mechanical actions quickly and accurately. As a new driver, especially if you are in your late teens, such thoughts will not bother you for a long time yet, but you still need to take account of the way it will affect those around you. Remember too that you can rarely identify the age of another driver: you simply see another Escort or Vectra or Volvo and assume the driver is just a driver.

You must take into account that all drivers are subject to a whole range of pressures all through their driving life. Ageing is only one of these. Ill health is not restricted to the elderly, of course; it affects many drivers; many people drive, ride, and concentrate badly when their health is below par. Premenstrual tension, for example, is a serious factor with very many women drivers, and three-quarters of vehicle accidents involving women take place in the particular week of their monthly cycles, when they are most affected by PMT. If this affects you, take note of its occurrence and make allowances when you plan long or difficult journeys. It is not only women who are affected by hormonal changes. Men suffer too, it's just that their cycles of inefficiency or maladroitness are not so predictable. Drivers of both sexes and all ages need to study their own lifestyles to find out what external and internal actions affect the way they think and drive.

FACT FILE

Stress affects everyone in one way or another.

If it affects your driving take your time and don't act hastily.

Stress affects others, so always make allowances for their mistakes.

The effects of ageing are often visible and predictable. But make allowances for those whose decision-making skills are below par for any reason.

Ill health is a serious driving matter.

If you are feeling ill, you should not drive.

If you must drive, then you need to do so with much more care than normally.

Q   How can I avoid stress when I am driving?
A   Put all your other worries behind you when you are driving.

Forget your non-driving worries until you are in a position to cope with them again.

Q   What if the stress and worries are to do with my driving?

A   Most new drivers are worried at some times during their training. Most driving stress is due to not understanding the vehicle, the route, or the conditions under which you are driving. Good instruction will reduce stress.

Q   Isn't driving a stressful occupation anyway?

A   Yes, but it is also one that you can control, provided you approach it safely and intelligently. If you are really worried about a driving situation, discuss it with your instructor and ask for help.

Q   How old does a driver have to be before ageing starts to affect their skills?

A   There is no fixed age. Some people are old at forty-five, others are still hale and hearty and good safe drivers well into their eighties. Safe driving is an attitude of mind.

Q   Is there anything a driver can do to counter the effects of ageing and ill health?

A   Yes. Concentrate on the driving task. If concentration becomes difficult keep to shorter journeys or take longer breaks.

Q   Is there anything a driver can do to take account of the effects of ageing and ill health in other road users?

A   Yes. Look out for signs of confusion or slowness in others and always make plenty of allowances for them.

3. Driving along the road

There are proper sequences needed before moving off and for following normal safe driving principles: these are easy to remember and put into operation the whole of the time you are on the road, but the only way this can be done is to carry them out every time you move off and drive, in order to make them part of your correct and safe hazard procedures for normal driving conditions. If you know and understand the reasons for them you are more likely to want to do them properly.

Put simply, it means recognizing and putting into practice every time you move off and drive the following sequences.

The first sequence is **moving off**.

Before you switch on the engine always check that the parking brake is applied, and the gear level is in neutral.

Before you move off check that the road behind is clear, that you can see where you are going, and that you will not interfere with other road users when you pull out into the stream of traffic.

Use your mirrors and check round over your shoulder for blind spots.

Check the road ahead and the mirrors again.

Only decide to move off if it is safe to do.

Signal if necessary (if anyone can benefit from the signal), clearly and precisely, and cancel the signal immediately it is of no use.

The next sequence is just as easy: **driving along**.

MIRRORS	Make full use of your mirrors – all of them – to make sure you know what is coming behind and over-taking you.
SIGNAL	Always decide if a signal is of any value to any other road user.
MANOEUVRE	The manoeuvre consists of three parts:
POSITION	Get into the correct position to carry out your next action.
SPEED	Adjust your speed to suit the action you are about to take, and make sure that you have selected the most suitable gear for that speed and action.
LOOK	Looking also consists of three separate stages:
LOOK	Take in as much information as you can.
ASSESS	Work out how this information will affect what you want to do.
DECIDE	Take the correct action, promptly and safely.

FACT FILE

Always keep left when driving along unless road signs indicate otherwise.

Only move out to the right if you want to overtake or turn. Even then you must look out for and give way to any oncoming traffic.

Avoid driving on the footpath or pavement.

Give way to horses or people with animals and allow adequate room for cyclists and other vulnerable road users.

Where there are lane markings, stay in the middle of your lane.

Follow a safety line at all times. This is normally about 1 metre (3 feet) from the gutter or any vehicle or other road user on your left.

When overtaking only do so if you can maintain at least a 1 metre gap.

When overtaking cyclists allow at least 2 metres (6 feet) for extra safety.

Q   Why do I need to check the parking brake and gear lever before starting the engine?

A   You must avoid starting the engine whilst in gear to avoid jerking the car forward or backward.

Q   Should I get ready to move off before I signal?

A   Yes, only signal you are moving off when you are completely ready.

Q   Should I release the parking brake before I signal to move off?

A   Not normally. Hold it with your left hand and only release it as the clutch comes up to start moving you off.

Q   When do I apply the M-S-M sequence?

A   In every manoeuvre that you carry out.

Q   What is a manoeuvre?

A   Anything and everything you do on the road.

Q   Does this mean I must signal for everything I do?

A   No, you only signal if it is helpful to any other road user.

Q   What does a manoeuvre consist of?

A   Anything which involves a change of speed and/or position.

Q   How do I signal that I am slowing down?

A   The normal way would be with the brake-lights. Each time you touch them they light up and warn other road users to be careful.

Q   Are brake-lights always good enough to warn people I am slowing or stopping?

A   No, they always come on after you have started to brake. Sometimes you will need to warn people *before* you start to brake or slow down.

Q   How do I signal that I am going to brake or slow down soon?

A   You can give an arm signal. It is clear and uncomplicated.

Q   What are the other benefits of arm signals?

A You can give the signal early, it is clear to people ahead of you, and you won't forget to cancel it.

Q What is a safety line?

A A safety line is the position about 1 metre (3 feet) from the kerb in the road along which you move.

Q How wide is the gap from other vehicles or does it vary?

A It means a gap of at least 1 metre (3 feet) from any vehicle on your left at 30 mph.

Q Why do I need to leave a gap for parked traffic?

A If anyone opens a door, you will see exactly how narrow 1 metre is – usually slightly less than a car door width.

Q What do I do about oncoming traffic on my right in busy narrow roads?

A If the traffic is heavy and you do not have a lot of room, you must drive more slowly.

Q What sort of gap do I leave on the right then?

A You should never be closer to oncoming traffic than to traffic on your left.

Q How do I position my car when driving in town in lanes with white lines to separate the parallel lines of traffic?

A This is easy; if you are in a lane, keep centrally positioned in it.

Q How do I cope with driving along a narrow busy road if I cannot allow a metre each side of me for safety?

A If the road is not wide enough to have a metre safety gap each side, you must drive more slowly. If you only have half a metre each side your speed should not exceed 15 mph.

Q How about cyclists, can I drive closer to them than I would to a car?

A No! You must allow even more room for cyclists, because they will often wobble or swerve to avoid drains and other obstacles.

Q Isn't it up to the cyclist to keep a straight course when I drive past them?

A No. Apart from anything else, they are susceptible to wind pressure as you rush past. Give them plenty of space.

Q Is it worse or better if two child cyclists are together?

A Potentially much more dangerous. Give them room to be foolish too.

4. Safe and correct coordination of controls

The correct coordination of clutch control – that is, using the accelerator and the clutch together rather than the handbrake whilst holding the car stationary on a hill – is one of the most fulfilling lessons you will ever learn. Learning to drive includes many skill operations, but the one which gives you the greatest sense of satisfaction is the knowledge that you can move off the car safely, and precisely, exactly when you want to.

The skill is to use the accelerator to get the engine speed up, select first gear if you are moving uphill forwards, and allow the clutch to come slowly up until the 'bite' of the clutch holds the wheels from rolling backwards. At that point you can release the handbrake (or parking brake) and the car won't move at all, either creeping up the hill or slipping down it.

Once you can do this you can drive anywhere.

The second coordination skill is similar because it also needs to combine using your left arm to change gear and your right arm to signal; perhaps before slowing down, or to add weight to an indicator: 'I really am going to slow down for this crossing' or 'I am actually turning right into this little entry over here'. This particular coordination skill is much more in the mind, however, because it is a question of getting plenty of time to carry out a sequence, without having to take both hands off the wheel whilst changing gear or to try to turn the steering-wheel with only one hand.

There is one more vehicle control coordination skill you will learn, but this one comes much later in your driving life. It is the skill to accelerate through and round bends smoothly, correctly, and safely.

FACT FILE

Clutch control enables you to manoeuvre the vehicle in confined spaces.

The only time you should slip the clutch is when you are manoeuvring.

The steeper the hill the more acceleration is needed to overcome it.

On level ground you may be able to move the car off without any acceleration – practise

> **this with your instructor occasionally to develop your clutch coordination control.**
>
> **Coordinated clutch control gives you the ability to drive and move off safely anywhere you wish.**

Q   Am I allowed to slip the clutch when driving?

A   No, you would normally only slip the clutch when manoeuvring in first or reverse gears.

Q   Where should I practise clutch control?

A   With your instructor you will practise it a lot in your early lessons.

Q   Will I need to practise it all the time I am driving, even after my lessons?

A   No, once you have learned the skill you won't need to practise it at all. You just do it automatically every time you move off or manoeuvre.

Q   Should I give hand signals when driving or are indicators better?

A   Arm signals for slowing down or stopping can be helpful, especially to other road users ahead.

Q   Should I use arm signals instead of indicators to say I am turning?

A   Not normally. Indicators are usually brighter and more easily seen.

Q   If I use an arm signal to slow down when approaching a pedestrian crossing how can I change gear to slow down as well?

A   You should not need to use the gears to slow down in a case like this. If the signal is more important, give that. But don't try to change gear as well.

Q   Does giving arm signals interfere with keeping both hands on the steering-wheel.

A   Yes, and this is why indicator switches are placed so conveniently. Only use an arm signal when you do not need to turn the steering-wheel.

Q   Should I give an arm signal when I move off?

A   Not normally, because you can indicate if you need and keep both hands on the steering-wheel. But giving an arm signal, as part of a lesson on moving off, can be a good indication to your instructor that you have proper coordination of clutch, accelerator, handbrake, and steering.

5. Correct safety sequences when approaching road and traffic hazards

The correct sequence for approaching the following hazards is usually the same that you used for moving along the road: M-S-M, P-S-L, and L-A-D.

The hazards include: turnings and junctions out from side roads (these can become crossroads when there are more than one at a time); roundabouts, which were often crossroads but now allow a better traffic flow; pedestrian crossings; traffic lights; traffic controllers; and other potential hazards. The noticeable difference is that when taking right and left turns, and going through roundabouts, crossroads, and traffic lights, the hazards are more obvious, predictable, and repetitive.

When turning left, first of all confirm to yourself where the left turn is. About ten seconds before you expect to arrive begin the first sequence of M-S-M.

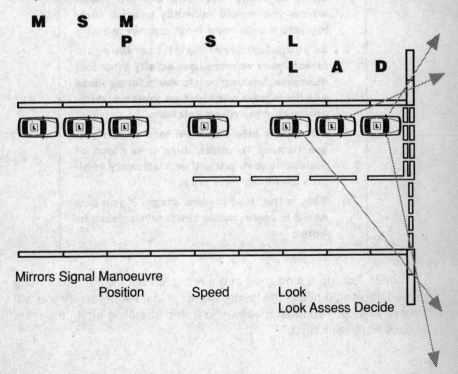

M   S   M
       P   S   L
                    L   A   D

Mirrors Signal Manoeuvre
          Position   Speed   Look
                                       Look Assess Decide

M This means that you check your mirrors again. In normal driving you always know who is behind you anyway, but because you have to know what signal you are about to give and who will benefit from it you need to make another specific mirrors check. Use all your mirrors, not just the centre one.

S The signal is normally a left indicator; confirm that it is correctly used. Then commence the left-turn manoeuvre, which will start by making sure that you maintain a course about 1 metre (3 feet) from the left gutter. This makes allowances for drains, etc. and will enable you to go round the corner without cutting in or swinging out.

S Your speed will need to be brought down to about 5 mph and the gear changed down to second. These figures do not apply to every left turn, but are those which you would normally use for turning into a side road from a main road.

L As you get closer to the left turn you again check your mirrors, especially your left door one, looking particularly for cyclists or others who might be on your nearside and in danger when you turn.

L Then look into the road into which you are turning to make sure it is clear of pedestrians or parked or stationary vehicles blocking your way.

A This is the assessment stage. If you can see it is clear, make the final decision to enter.

When leaving a side road and turning left out from it into a main road, the sequence is the same, except that it's more likely you will need to stop. You must give way to traffic travelling along the main road from your right.

Approach as before, using mirrors and signal, position, speed and gears correctly selected. It is more likely that the speed for entering a main road from the left would be about 2–3 mph, and in first gear. You look to the right as you reach a point about the middle of the five hazard-warning lines in the centre of your road. If it seems clear, look to the left in order to assess the situation again.

Turning right into a side road means crossing the path of any oncoming traffic. Turning right from a side road means that you have to cross that first half of the road. However, you must also make sure it is safe to join the traffic coming on your left. In each case the same sequence and assessments are weighed up before any decision is made.

FACT FILE

Turning left and right involves giving way to other traffic and road users.

If you follow the M-S-M, P-S-L, L-A-D sequence you will always be safe.

The priority sequence for traffic at a junction is:

1. turning left into a side road: only give way to people in their lane as you turn;

2. turning left out: also give way to any traffic on your right as you turn;

3. turning right in: also give way to traffic coming towards you before you cross their path;

4. turning right out: you must give way to everyone else.

Whenever you are turning into or out from a road, always be prepared to give way to cyclists and especially pedestrians who may be crossing near you.

Pedestrians crossing the road must have priority at all times.

Q   If I am turning left into a side road should I always give way to pedestrians waiting at the kerb?

A   If they are waiting and the road is clear for you to drive round the corner you should do so. If you are not sure, wait and go slow enough to stop.

Q   What do I do if the pedestrians have started to cross?

A   Allow them to finish crossing safely and without harassment.

Q   Should I wave them across?

A   No. Waving is not a proper signal, and by doing it the pedestrians might not bother to look to see if other traffic is also letting them cross.

Q   How should I help pedestrians who are waiting to cross the road?

A   Usually the best way is to get out of their way, unless there is a lot of traffic or there is a proper crossing for them.

Q   At traffic lights when I am waiting at a red light can I help pedestrians to cross?

A   Most traffic lights have a pedestrian crossing built in. Do not wait in this area.

Q   When I am emerging at a left turn into a busy road, can I creep out?

A   You ought to wait until you can emerge without causing any other road user, even cyclists, to brake or swerve to avoid you.

Q   What is the best way to make sure it is clear and safe to emerge?

A   You need to make eye contact with every road user who can give you priority.

Q   Is it all right just to look to the left and right before I emerge?

A   No, the correct sequence is to look right first, then left, then right again. You have to continue looking both ways until you are sure it is safe to emerge.

Q   How about crossroads where I have priority – do I need to look there?

A   Yes, it is not enough to have priority, you need to see that others are going to give it to you.

Q   What is the difference between right of way and priority?

A   Priority exists on most road situations, and white lines and other signs tell you whether you have it or not. Right of way is a legal term and gives the impression that you can go at any time without checking. The Department of Transport will not use the words right of way for this reason.

Q   When I am turning right into a main road do I still need to look to the right first?

A   Yes, you look right to see if there is any traffic coming towards you. If it is apparently clear you then look left to see what traffic is coming towards you that way. Only then can you think about assessing and making decisions.

Q   Can I cross in front if an oncoming car flashes its lights when I
    am turning right?
A   No, wait until the driver shows obvious signs of slowing down –
    a headlight flash doesn't mean you can go. Make sure it's
    absolutely safe before you cross its path.
Q   What does a headlight flash mean when I am waiting to cross or
    emerge?
A   A flashing headlight only draws attention to the presence of a
    vehicle. It cannot be considered as an invitation.
Q   Can I wait in the middle of a central reservation when I am
    turning right?
A   Only if you can make sure the whole of your vehicle is safely
    inside it.
Q   What happens if I push my way across the road in busy traffic?
A   You must not do it; and if you risk it you could be responsible for
    an accident, and the consequent claims or court decisions.
Q   Is turning right dangerous?
A   No, but if you don't follow the rules you can make it dangerous.
    The rules are made to be obeyed and keep all road users,
    including yourself, safe at all times.

6. The principles involved in braking distances, stopping correctly, smoothly, and safely, and in the selection of safe stopping places

As a driver you must always know the rules regarding stopping,
waiting, and parking.

Stopping
Stopping is not parking: you remain with or in the vehicle. You might
stop very briefly, to load passengers or pick up some goods, you
might need to wait with the engine switched off. In all cases you can
keep an eye open to ensure that you are not causing any traffic
congestion or breaking any of the rules contained in the Highway
Code, paragraphs 137–146.

Waiting
If you are waiting at the edge of the road, perhaps to pick up
someone or something, you are still governed by rules and regulations. Some roads, such as red routes, do not allow you to stop or
wait at all on them. Similarly you may not stop or wait on motorways
except in proper service areas or in emergencies.

Parking

Parking, which means locking and leaving your vehicle, should only be done in acceptable, safe, and authorized parking places. A parking place is a designated area either at the edge of the carriageway or off-road, where you are allowed to leave your vehicle legally and with reasonable safety from being hit by passing traffic. Always read the times and regulations which cover any particular parking site and comply with them. Remember that if you park in an unauthorized area you may well find your vehicle clamped or towed away when you return.

FACT FILE

You must not park where there are red or yellow lines along the edge of the carriageway, except in accordance with times and details displayed.

You must not park or wait on the approach to a pedestrian crossing.

You must not park on a signed school entrance during stated times.

You must not park or wait on a clearway or a motorway.

You must not park in a residents' or disabled parking bay.

You must not park at night facing the wrong direction.

You must not stop or wait on roads with double white lines down the centre even if the broken line is on your side.

You should not park where you could inconvenience other road users.

You should not park within 10 metres (33 feet) of a junction.

You should not park in front of the entrance to someone's property.

You should not park or wait near the brow of a hill or humpback bridge.

Q What are the rules about parking, waiting, and stopping?
A You should not stop or park your vehicle where it would cause inconvenience or danger to other road users. Nor must you park in any of the designated areas which prohibit parking.
Q What are the rules about obstruction?
A Under the Highways Act 1834, obstruction of the highway at any time or place is an offence unless the driver can show that parking or waiting is actually allowed there.
Q Does that mean I can be prosecuted for obstruction even if there are no 'no parking' signs?
A Yes. Parking is an obstruction unless it is specifically allowed.
Q Am I allowed to park without lights at night?
A Parking without lights is allowed for car drivers provided it is on a road with a 30 mph or less speed limit, facing the correct way, and not within 10 metres (33 feet) of the end of the road.
Q Can I stop on an urban clearway to pick up passengers?
A Yes, this is the difference between stopping and waiting. You can pick up passengers in this situation.
Q Can I park my car and caravan on the road without lights at night?
A No. A caravan or a trailer must be lit with proper parking or sidelights at night.
Q What other vehicles are not allowed to park without lights at night?
A Large goods vehicles and any vehicles over 1,525 kilograms (1.5 tons) unladen are not allowed to park without lights, nor are vehicles with projecting loads.
Q What is a Red Route?
A This is a special series of roads through some large towns where the lines at the edge of the pavement are painted red instead of yellow. No stopping, waiting, or parking is allowed on these roads at the times shown on signs.
Q If I am parked unsafely can I use hazard-warning lights to tell other road users?
A The simple answer is yes, but the safest answer is not to park unsafely. Hazard lights are to warn of dangers, not to excuse bad or inconvenient parking.
Q Are there any special rules about parking next to or near to a disabled driver's vehicle?

A   Yes, remember that they may not be able to get proper access to their vehicle if you are too close to them. Some disabled drivers need easy wheelchair access.
Q   When I park at the side of the road, what precautions am I expected to take with regard to children who are passengers?
A   Make sure they get out of the car on the pavement side. Do not allow them to open doors without checking it is safe to do so.
Q   What safety precautions must I take when I park and leave the vehicle?
A   Always switch off the engine, apply the handbrake, and lock all doors securely.
Q   Are there any added security provisions I should take?
A   Yes, put all your goods out of sight or in the boot. Do not tempt thieves.

7. The effect of weather and road conditions on the road-holding capabilities of your car or motor cycle

There are many risk factors related to various road conditions that you are likely to meet every day; they will change according to the time of year and time of day. In particular, you must be aware of the increased dangers of skidding due to poor tyre grip when the roads are wet or greasy. Each tyre on your vehicle only has a footprint the size of a small shoe. This is the only contact you have with the road surface. If anything weakens that grip you can easily lose control of your vehicle with disastrous results.

You may be aware of loss of grip because you can feel it through your steering-wheel or handlebars. But this is usually too late to be able to do anything about it. If the roads are wet, especially if it has recently rained after a long dry spell, you can anticipate the conditions becoming difficult and adjusting your driving to suit. Always drive more slowly in the rain or when the roads are greasy. Autumn leaves on the road also make roads as treacherous as if they were icy. Learn to look all year round and make sure that you can always slow down safely in the distance you can see to be safe. When driving on bad road surfaces you need to make maximum use of your observation and perception to avoid getting into trouble.

FACT FILE

Skids are always caused by people, not vehicles, tyres, ice, or luck.

In order of importance, skids are avoided by sensible drivers, tyres in good condition, and good road surfaces.

Good drivers with good tyres can cope with bad road conditions.

Drivers' reaction times are more important than anything else.

Drivers can improve their reaction times by concentrating on what they are doing.

Q   What causes skidding?
A   Excessive speed, excessive braking, or excessive steering for the available tyre grip.
Q   How can I avoid skidding?
A   Drive at a safe speed suitable for the road and surface conditions. Keep your tyres in good condition and make sure they have enough tread to disperse any surface water.
Q   How can I improve my reaction times?
A   Concentrate on the road ahead, but also try to perceive what is likely to happen. Plan your driving and always know you can stop in the distance you can see to be safe.
Q   Why are dry roads especially bad when it first starts to rain?
A   The long dry spells build up a surface of rubber dust and oil which fills the cracks in the road. These then mix with the water of the first showers to make a greasy surface.
Q   Why does this only last a short time?
A   Once a heavy rainfall has washed the roads clean, the surface is quite good again.
Q   What other road surfaces can become greasy?
A   Anything which forms a layer between the road surface and your tyres can make it difficult for the tyres to grip. This is why good tyre tread is needed to match your driving attention.
Q   Should I lower my tyre pressures when driving on icy roads?
A   No, never reduce your tyre pressures for ice, snow, or any other reason. Driving on lower tyre pressures than are recommended for your vehicle is illegal.

Q Do bad road conditions make it more difficult to stop in an emergency?

A Yes, obviously bad road surfaces make it more difficult to stop. This is why your braking distances are much greater in bad weather. The answer is to drive more slowly, and give yourself much more room from any hazards ahead when the weather is bad.

8. Other factors making driving difficult

Road surfaces are not the only things that change. Drivers and other road users will experience changes in their own behaviour which may be due to the influence of alcohol, drugs, or medicaments. Some drugs can be helpful: for instance hay fever sufferers can actually be safer if they take their recommended drugs; but aspirin, paracetamol, and many cough medicines act on the driver's reaction and thinking times. Anything which causes a driver to react more slowly must be considered a danger.

It is not only medicines, of course. A driver's state of mind has a tremendous effect on driving behaviour. Even if you are feeling fatigued or tired you must not allow this to interfere with your driving attention. Anything which decreases your attention increases your risk of accident, injury, and death. Road users who are very young or suffering from some of the effects of old age will also be more at risk. Your responsibility towards them is even greater.

Even though you may not have been driving for very long, there will still be other road users with even less experience than you have. And many of those who have been driving longer may still not have the same powers of attention which you can give. The irrationality of other road users, especially in the very young and very old age groups, is something you must accept and make full allowances for: pedestrians, children, adolescents, and the elderly and infirm are in the greatest danger; you must treat them as specific risk groups.

There are many patterns of predictability for certain groups of road users which with practice and skill you can discover and use to your advantage, but there is also a lack of consistency in some road users' behaviour which you need to know about and make allowances for. You must also be aware of the increased accident risk caused by the specific driving characteristics of various types of vehicles, and the need for different paths to be taken by other vehicles when turning. Large trucks, especially rigid ones, take a much wider path than you do, and articulated trucks take a different path again. Look at how much room they need and see how you must keep well clear of them when they are turning.

FACT FILE

One of the worst features of the effects of alcohol on drivers is that it gives them a sense of over-confidence.

Drinking alcohol seriously affects driving skills and judgement.

The previous night's drinking can still leave you over the limit next morning.

The breath-test limit is 35 microgrammes per millilitre of breath.

The blood-test limit is 80 milligrammes per millilitre of blood.

The urine-test limit is 107 milligrammes per millilitre of urine.

A second drink-drive offence within ten years carries a minimum disqualification period of three years.

The very young, the elderly, and the infirm must all be accorded added care.

Larger vehicles need to take wider paths especially when turning.

Accidents do not happen; they are always caused – and 95% are the driver's fault.

Accident risk is increased when drivers are careless, but some road users are involved in many more accidents than others.

Speed does not cause accidents, but it increases the effect dramatically.

All accidents can be avoided if drivers and riders take care.

Q   Can a small sherry or a glass of wine affect my driving performance?

A   Any amount of alcohol must have some effect. Perhaps the worst effect is that it makes you careless.

Q   If I am found guilty of drink driving what is the result?

A   It is not only the criminal offence and punishment. You could lose your licence and be required to attend a drink counselling service, but just as serious is the fact that it is very difficult for convicted drink drivers to get insurance cover again. The cost can be enormous.

Q   Is this the most serious result of drink driving?

A   No, the most serious effect is killing a passer-by. Can you live with that?

Q   Why are adolescents a danger on the road, since they are quite quick to react?

A   They often react quickly without thinking. Most youngsters have no experience of the speed of traffic or the effect of being struck by a vehicle.

Q   Are motor cyclists more at risk than car drivers?

A   Yes. Regardless of who is to blame, if a motor cyclist is hit they have no safety cage around them to protect them. Falling off a bike at speed is serious in itself.

Q   Why do large trucks take such large turning circles?

A   They have much longer wheelbases and heavy loads to get round.

Q   Should I overtake a large truck going round a roundabout?

A   No, even if you think you can squeeze through, you don't know what the driver is planning to do.

Q   If I overtake a large truck how should I get past – quickly or slowly?

A   Get past as soon as you can, because you may well be in the driver's blind spots.

Q   Is there anything else I should remember about driving behind large trucks?

A   Yes, don't follow too closely. Unladen trucks with very good brakes can stop quite quickly and if the driver cannot see you, you might slide right underneath his trailer.

Q   Are accidents involving heavy trucks worse than those involving cars?

A   Yes, unfortunately the weight of large trucks is such that they keep on going when they hit something.

9. What you do if accidents do happen

Drivers need to know what to do if they are involved in any accident, and they ought to know what to do if they arrive at the scene of someone else's. First of all there is an absolute rule that if you are involved in any accident, regardless of how minor or negligible it may seem, you must stop. Failing to stop is a serious motoring offence. You are also obliged to give all the details required to anyone who has reasonable cause to see them.

In practice this means that if your car is involved in a bump with another car you must exchange names and addresses with the other driver, and if necessary give the names and addresses of the registered keepers (or owners) of the vehicles. For example you could be in your driving instructor's car, the registered keeper of which is a large national driving school. (The owner's name is not so important, the vehicle may be leased and therefore owned by a finance company.)

If for any reason you are unable to exchange these details – if the other vehicle fails to stop, for example – then you must report in person to the police as soon as possible. In any event it must be reported within twenty-four hours. Please note that this does not mean you have twenty-four hours in which to report the accident, the law requires you to report the incident as soon as possible.

The driver of a vehicle leaving the scene of an accident can be charged with the offences of failing to stop and failing to exchange details, and therefore it is vital that you do stop after any incident. If a lone female fears that the accident may have been contrived to make her stop her car and get out, there is a legal loophole for her: she can drive immediately and directly to the nearest police station in order to report the incident and her fears, and there is little likelihood that any prosecution for failing to stop will follow.

If there is any personal injury involved then details of the insurance certificate should also be exchanged. One of the problems with motor accidents is that some injuries – whiplash injuries to the neck, for instance – are not immediately apparent. When asked if you are injured or hurt in any way you should not reply that you are perfectly all right if there is any danger that later on you may suffer from the effects of the crash. Even when there is no injury and only the slightest damage to either vehicle you are still required to follow these procedures. These responsibilities apply regardless of who was responsible for the incident, and even if you assume very little actual damage has been done you may still find out later that the cost of repairs may be more than you expected.

The scene of the accident is not the best place to work out who was to blame, although you do need to ask any witnesses for their names and addresses in case you need their evidence later. If the person who hit you is willing to admit responsibility get them to sign something to that effect and your insurance company will be delighted. Their insurers won't though, and you must never, ever, in any circumstances, admit an incident was your fault. Apart from any legal consequences, by doing so you may be absolving your own insurance company from payment for damages and have to pay it all yourself.

If there is any doubt about the accident the police and any other emergency services should be called. The police will not normally attend to bumper-touch types of accidents, but if you really want them to attend, you can truthfully answer that you don't know when they ask if anyone was injured. You might find out you have been later.

An accident does not have to involve any other vehicle, of course. You may clip a bollard, reverse into a lamppost or other street furniture, or hit something in the road. This is still an accident if any damage was caused or if anyone could have grounds for compensation or make a claim against you. The law requires the accident to be reported even when no other vehicle is involved if damage or injury is caused to anyone else, their property, or to certain specified types of animals: cattle, horses, donkeys, and mules; sheep, pigs and goats, and dogs. If animals not on this list are the only things involved it is not necessary to report it. However if a cat is killed or injured and the owner can be found you should do your best to find them and explain what happened.

If you arrive at the scene of an accident you must make a rapid decision to stop and assist, or to keep going. You may also have to think about reporting the accident if you feel it would help, but keep out of the way if you are unable to be of assistance.

First Aid on the road
If you have first-aid training and know how to use any first-aid kit carried in your vehicle, offer your services to whoever seems to be in charge. Do not rush in with help unless you really know what to

do. If you carry a kit in your car learn how to use it by taking a short first-aid course. Many first-aid kits are not very comprehensive. If you do take training make sure that the kit you carry contains all the recommended items.

FACT FILE

Know how to deal with accidents when they occur.

Keep your own car safe and out of danger.

Warn other traffic, possibly by use of hazard-warning lights.

Switch off all vehicle engines and put out any cigarettes.

Ensure that someone has called the emergency services.

Give full details of the location, number of vehicles, and any possible injuries.

Assist road-accident victims but do not move them unless they are in immediate danger. Know what first aid you can give, or ask someone else to.

Move the uninjured away from the actual scene of further danger.

Wait until the police or other emergency services have arrived and taken charge.

Be aware of extra dangers if any vehicle is carrying hazardous loads.

FACT FILE

If you are first to arrive at a roadside accident, or the only one prepared to carry out first-aid assistance:

It is crucial to make an accurate assessment of the injury situation.

Decide on the priorities of any treatment to any injured people at the scene.

Check airways and breathing first. If breathing is not present commence artificial ventilation.

Check for bleeding and control it. If necessary plug wounds with clothes.

Keep casualties warm and still. Try to keep them calm and to avoid shock.

Get others to assist, even if you keep them occupied to prevent interference.

Await ambulance, police or paramedics for specific action.

Q   If I am involved in an accident what is the first thing I must do?

A   Stop and exchange necessary details with anyone who has a right to know.

Q   What do I do if the other driver is to blame but won't admit it?

A   Ignore this at the time, but give your insurance company full details plus the names of any witnesses.

Q   Must I tell my insurance company if I am involved in an accident?

A   Yes – it is essential that you do in case you are involved in any future claims.

Q   Can I still keep my no-claims bonus if I tell them?

A   Yes, provided no claim is made and paid on your behalf. But remember a no-claims bonus is not a no-blame bonus.

Q   Can I lose my no-claims bonus if the other driver doesn't admit responsibility?

A   You can lose your no-claims bonus if anyone makes a claim on your insurance. This includes you making a claim yourself.

Q   What should I do if I have an accident and it is blocking the traffic from moving?

A   If you can move your vehicles away from the actual scene of the incident to a safer place try to do this. But it may be necessary for someone to make measurements or to assess responsibility and this cannot always be done properly if the cars are moved.

Q   Should I try to direct the traffic around the scene whilst waiting for the police to arrive?

A   Someone may have to do this, but it must be done safely and properly. The first rule of any accident has to be to safeguard the scene and prevent further accidents.

Q Should I take any photographs of the scene after the incident?

A It is always an advantage if you have photographs or good drawings of what happened. If you do this, try to get corroborative evidence of witnesses too.

Q Will my insurance company pay for all the damage to other vehicles and property?

A If you are properly insured the main insurance cover you will have is for third-party damage. This means they will pay for any one else's damage to be repaired or replaced, if it was caused by your vehicle.

Q Will my insurance company pay for all the damage to my own vehicle?

A This depends on the type of insurance you have. If you have comprehensive cover you may still be liable to pay an 'excess' charge – perhaps the first £50 or £100 of the total damage.

Q If my vehicle is damaged will my insurance company pay for a hire car whilst mine is being repaired?

A This isn't normally covered by your own insurers if the accident was your fault. But you need to check your own insurance to see what it actually covers. You will only get the insurance cover you ask for and pay for.

Q If the other driver is at fault will their insurance company pay for a hire car whilst mine is being repaired?

A If the other driver or their insurance company admit liability for the incident then you can claim for all legitimate expenses which you incur. Keep a list of all your costs.

Q If I am driving along a dual carriageway and I see an accident on the other side what should I do?

A Normally keep driving and avoid rubber-necking – this is often the cause of secondary accidents. If you genuinely believe you can help, pull off the road where it is safe and suitable and see if you can assist. Otherwise drive on.

Q If I am first at the scene of a serious traffic accident what is the first thing I should do?

A Stop, pull off the road if you can. Safeguard the scene and send for assistance.

Q If I am stopped at the scene of an accident and cannot help what should I do?

A Keep your car safe and avoid getting in the way of others who are helping.

Q   If I have first-aid training should I offer my services?

A   Yes, but check that the police and other emergency services have been called.

Q   If anyone is injured should I help to move them from their cars?

A   It depends on the incident. If there is a greater danger from fire or further collisions then it may be necessary to move them, but avoid moving injured people and making their injuries worse.

Q   If a motor cyclist has been knocked from his bike should I take off his helmet?

A   No. You should never remove an injured motor cyclist's helmet. It is common practice to fit neck and collar restraints on all accident victims. A crash helmet can help.

Q   Is it a good idea to carry a first-aid kid in a family car?

A   Yes. But make sure it is a good one. Most cheap first-aid kits are not much help at all.

Q   Where should I keep a first-aid kit?

A   The best place is inside the body of the car, not locked in the boot. Make sure that it is not just lying loose on the back shelf. You don't want to need it for injuries caused by flying first-aid kits.

Q   Is it a good idea to take first-aid training?

A   All road users need to have some basic knowledge of first aid. You cannot rely on a nurse or doctor being on the scene.

Q   What knowledge of first aid would I need to assist at the scene of an accident?

A   Be prepared to let anyone with more experience take charge. But if you are alone, there is a simple ABC of first aid which anyone can apply.

Q   What is the ABC system of first aid?

A   First of all make sure that accident victims have an open AIRWAY.
Secondly check that they are BREATHING.
Finally ensure they have good CIRCULATION (that they still have a pulse).

Q   What other steps should I then take if no one else is assisting at the scene of an accident?

A   Having checked that breathing is normal, check for any severe bleeding and control it. Then place any unconscious victims in the 'Recovery Position'. But do not move anyone unless you are certain there is no possibility of any spinal or internal injury.

Q What other steps can I take to assist with first aid at the scene of an accident?
A Take a good first-aid course; carry an efficient first-aid kit; and offer your services if they are needed.

10. Breakdown procedures

Drivers also need to know the safety procedures to be followed in the case of vehicle breakdowns on the road, both for themselves and for other road users. They need to know about stopping in real emergencies, and how to recognize when a real emergency has arisen and what to do about it. They must also understand that most of these can be avoided and should also know how to avoid emergencies developing unnecessarily.

Although punctures, blow-outs, and other incidents can occur spontaneously, there is always an underlying cause which could have been avoided. In many cases good servicing and regular checks will give early warning of wear and tear. The potential for creating incidents can be limited by taking care not to bump the kerb or cause other forms of tyre damage. Nevertheless every driver should know how to change a wheel, and it's a good idea to get some practice in a good dry safe place. The worst possible places to learn how to do this for the first time are on a miserable lonely road in the rain at night, or on a motorway hard shoulder in bad visibility.

This is one very useful practical lesson that your professional driving instructor would be delighted to give you. It only takes ten minutes or so in good conditions if you have all the right equipment available, but that could be the longest hour of your life if the circumstances are wrong. The wheel-changing equipment in a new car is adequate, but you may not have all of it in a second-hand car, and the best tool-kit in the world is not much help if you don't know how to use it properly. Your driving instructor could also advise you on the best additional equipment that you should carry in your car once you are driving on your own after the test.

FACT FILE

Make use of an advance warning triangle if you have one.

Use your hazard lights to warn other road users.

If you are able to move the car, get off the road or find a safer place to wait.

Get any passengers out of the car and into a safe place.

If you cannot repair the vehicle quickly contact a breakdown service.

Get police help if you are causing an obstruction.

Do not try to change a wheel yourself if there is any possible danger.

Get help to control the traffic if possible. But don't ask for help from strangers.

Never try to change a wheel on the hard shoulder of any motorway. Call in the professionals.

Q   What is the distance that an advance warning triangle should be placed on a motorway or dual carriageway?

A   150 metres (164 yards) behind the incident.

Q   What is the distance that an advance warning triangle should be used on an ordinary single carriageway road?

A   On a straight level road about 50 metres (55 yards).

Q   What if the road bends or is on a hill?

A   On a winding or hilly road the triangle should be placed before the bends or hill starts.

Q   What are the main causes of vehicle breakdowns?

A   Neglect, failing to make regular vehicle checks and services, and abuse of the vehicle.

Q   What is meant by 'abuse of the vehicle'?

A   Driving for long distances for too long. Driving at high revs or too fast over bumpy road surfaces, and scraping tyres against kerbs and other obstructions. And of course not having regular checks and servicing.

Q   What can disabled drivers do when their vehicles break down?

A   They should display a special HELP sign from their windows or in an open boot.

Q   What can I do to help if I see a disabled driver in a broken-down vehicle?

A   Stop and park safely and ask if you can assist in any way, or call someone.

Q   If I break down on a motorway are there any ways to get help?

A   Yes, there are special telephones every mile along each motor-way. Walk to the nearest and you will be given guidance on what to do. Park on the hard shoulder, but get passengers out of the vehicle and across the barrier.

Q   Isn't it dangerous for a female driver to wait outside the car when broken down?

A   The dangers of being hit from behind by a dozing driver are much much greater than of being harassed or attacked by someone. If there is any peculiar threat get back in until that particular danger has gone.

Q   What does it feel like to have a front tyre burst on me whilst driving along?

A   Your car will pull suddenly to one side. Keep a firm grip on the wheel and make sure it does not drag you across any traffic.

Q   What does it feel like to have a rear tyre burst whilst driving?

A   The rear of the car starts to sway from side to side. Hold the wheel firmly until you are able to slow down and pull over to a safe place.

Q   What happens if my brakes fail when I am driving along?

A   Unless you are in an emergency stop situation, go through each gear in turn using the clutch and gears to slow you down. Pulling the handbrake up momentarily will help to lock the rear wheels; but try not to lock the handbrake on.

Q   What happens if my brakes fail and I am aiming at stationary traffic?

A   Look for an alternative target you can sideswipe – like a hedge or fence. That way you can stop more slowly, and avoid a head-on smash.

Q   What should I do if I get a puncture in a tyre on the driver's side on a motorway?

A   Never even think about changing a wheel in this situation. Get one of the motoring associations to assist.

Q   If I do change my wheel myself are there any particular precautions I should take?

A   Yes. Make sure the brakes are properly on. Chock the wheels if need be. Try to work on a level surface, away from passing traffic, and with someone to guard you. Make sure you tighten all the wheel nuts up properly afterwards.

Q   How can I make sure my spare wheel is suitable in case of a puncture?

A   Check the state of your spare tyre regularly, that is at least once a week, and make sure you can get at it easily. Do you know how it is fixed? Find out and remember.

Q   Should I use my hazard-warning lights if I am broken down on the road?

A   Yes, this is the only reason that they are fitted. Use them if they will act as a warning to other road users, and keep traffic from running into you.

11. Vehicle manoeuvres and parking

There are a number of manoeuvres and exercises you must carry out on your driving test, and you will also need to do most of them regularly in your normal day to day driving. The manoeuvring exercises you must be able to do include: reversing in a straight line, reversing around corners, turning in the road, parking at the kerbside, and parking in parking places. You must also understand the numerous parking regulations and restrictions and the various road markings and signs governing parking.

There are a few questions you should ask yourself before you commence any manoeuvre which involves crossing the path of other traffic, or doing anything which may be unexpected. These questions are simple and you need to answer each one with a positive yes before you start. If you cannot answer yes to any one of them, find somewhere else to do the exercise.

Ask yourself:

● Is this manoeuvre safe?

● Is it being done in a convenient place?

● Is it legal at this place?

● Am I able to complete the manoeuvre safely?

You will need to know the Highway Code and use your own experience, common sense, and the ability to look at it from another road user's point of view before you can say yes to all of them. If you can, then do it, quickly, safely, but with full recognition of everyone else's needs as well.

Reversing
Learn how to reverse in easy stages.

Reversing in a straight line
This is the simplest exercise. You need to sit so that you can see properly behind you, know which way to hold and steer the wheel, and how to move off under control using the accelerator and clutch. You also need to remember that if you are driving backwards, other vehicles might be taken by surprise by your actions so you have to look behind you just as much as you would use your mirrors when driving forwards.

Reversing to the left or right
This is just like reversing in a straight line except you fit in an extra bit, turning the steering-wheel left or right in the middle. Some learners worry about which way to turn the wheel, but practical experience soon convinces them that they don't have to worry about it at all. You steer the wheel left for left turns and right for right turns, exactly the same as going forwards. What you do have to do is avoid swinging round in the seat just to look at the steering-wheel. That is dangerous.

Turning in the road
This is the one driving manoeuvre which is really artificial. Indeed in Germany and some other countries it is regarded as an illegal manoeuvre, with no purpose in it. From a driving test point of view, however, drivers must be able to demonstrate their ability to move safely in a confined space both forwards and backwards, and this exercise is used to prove it. It has its equivalent when parking in a busy car park, but it can be done on a driving test without danger to nearby cars.

Parking at the kerbside
This must be the commonest exercise that you will ever do. Not every parking manoeuvre will involve reversing, of course, but by being able to reverse you give yourself many more opportunities to get into tighter parking spots.

All these reversing exercises are tested in the practical driving test. The final one, which is not specifically tested then, is the one that matters most: parking in recognized parking bays. However it's often asked for by the driving examiner at the end of the driving test, so it's even more necessary than learning how to reverse around the corners which are used on the test. In order to be a safe and competent driver you must be able to park your car wherever and whenever you need.

FACT FILE

Reversing is not difficult, but it does need skill, practice, and understanding to do it well.

You need to remember which way the steering-wheel turns, and the effect it will have.

You need to move the car slowly when manoeuvring, using clutch and accelerator pedals.

You need to check your observation points very carefully.

And you should stop the exercise if anyone else gets close to you.

Q Do I need to wear my seat-belt when reversing?

A No, seat-belts can be removed during any driving manoeuvre which involves reversing.

Q How should I sit when reversing?

A At an angle in your seat, so that it is natural to see out of the back window. It is not enough to be able to look through the side windows, you must be able to see properly behind you.

Q Should I hold the steering-wheel at the ten and two position when reversing?

A Not if it is more comfortable to hold it at the twelve and six or other positions. You must be comfortable, but you must be safe, and you must be able to turn the wheel effectively.

Q Can I reverse using my mirrors?

A You can, but you cannot see enough to be safe. Mirrors should only be used to confirm that what you are doing is correct, and not as direct means of vision.

Q What should I do if I am reversing and a car comes up behind me?

A Either stop and wait, or move back to where you started from.

Q   What should I do if I am turning in the road and a car flashes its lights at me?

A   Lights flashed only have one meaning – to draw attention to a vehicle's presence. Wait and see – if the car comes through, let it. If it waits for you, continue with your manoeuvre.

Q   How can I tell if a parking space is big enough for me?

A   A gap two cars long is ample for anyone to drive in. A car and a half length needs reversing into, and a car and a quarter needs skill.

Q   How do I know which way to steer when I am reversing?

A   Don't look at the wheel. If you are reversing around to the left, steer left. If to the right, steer right.

Q   How can I control my speed when I am manoeuvring?

A   Use the accelerator at steady throttle, and keep your foot on the clutch and slip it slightly, so that your speed is as slow as you want it to be.

Q   Where should I look when I am reversing?

A   Always look at what you want to hit as you go to where you look. Better still, look at where you want to finish up.

Q   When do I look to the front when reversing?

A   Just before you start, before you swing your front out as you turn the wheel, and to confirm that it is still safe behind you.

Q   Is it a good idea to use a drawing pin in the rear window rubber as a sight guide?

A   No, for two reasons. One is that you won't always have a car with a pin; and more importantly, if you are looking at a drawing pin you won't see where you are going.

Q   Should I get out and walk round the car before I reverse?

A   It is not necessary if you have just driven forwards before reversing. But if you are getting into your car after an interval you must be sure it is safe behind you, so then you should.

Q   How far am I allowed to reverse in a car?

A   The answer in the Highway Code is always given as a reasonable distance. Only a policeman or a court could define what is reasonable at any particular time and place. The answer is not to reverse further than is necessary, nor enough to inconvenience anyone else.

12. Ways of controlling traffic

Speed limits are used as one means of controlling traffic. Limits must be obeyed because those who disregard them are also disregarding the safety, convenience, and comfort of all other road users. If the authorities have agreed that a particular speed limit is needed for any road it is because there is obviously a good reason for it. Speed limits always have a purpose. Drivers who break speed limits are not only antisocial, they can easily get penalty points and heavy fines and lose their driving licence. All of which means that speeding is unnecessary, unsafe, and never worth the risk. If you are in a hurry, leave for your destination earlier.

The national speed limit in rural areas is normally 60 mph and for dual carriageways and motorways it is 70 mph. But speed limits must also take into account the type of vehicle and their purpose. Trucks and coaches are banned from some roads by virtue of their size, and they are also limited by speed and from certain lanes on motorways.

Built-up areas are normally subject to a 30 mph speed limit, although in some cases this can be reduced to a lower limit. Residential areas outside towns often have a 40 mph limit, and this is imposed because many house owners need to reverse or drive out of their garages onto the roads themselves. Higher speed limits here would make life quite difficult and probably dangerous for those residents.

Other forms of traffic management are used in many towns and cities. Full use is made of traffic lights, one-way streets, and large and small roundabouts. They are all used as a means of helping traffic flow. In a similar way, out in the country clearways are often used as a means to help drivers get the best out of road and traffic situations. The whole system of traffic signs and road markings is designed to help drivers, riders, and even pedestrians to make the best use of the roads we have.

Drivers and riders need to play their part in the system of traffic management by making sure that they take every opportunity to help with traffic flow. They can also assist with this by noting and obeying all the signs, warnings, and instructions given to them, and by making sure that they use intelligent signalling to other road users by arm, vehicle position, and indicator.

Signals and other signs given by other road users also help us to make our decisions and we must always be able to act on signals seen and implied by non-authorized means. This does not mean you have to go simply because another driver flashes his lights at you, but you must be able to make intelligent and safe decisions based on what you know, what you can see, and what you have been told.

The best way to do this is always to maintain proper eye contact with other road users so that you are sure you are both fully aware of each other's presence and intentions. This enables you to carry out intelligent and safe hazard perception and identification, and ultimately hazard avoidance. By following safe road procedures you will minimize dangers and know that you are playing your part in the traffic-management systems which need to exist for all road users to benefit.

FACT FILE

Speed limits and road signs are always there for a purpose.

Traffic flows smoothly and safely if all traffic in the same lane travels at the same speed.

Speed alone does not kill, but accidents at speed are more disastrous.

Road and traffic signs play a vital role in communications – but you must read, understand, and obey them for the system to work properly.

You can signal your intentions easily by arm, indicator, and position, but you must signal early – before you do something, not just during.

Speed limits are the maximum, not a target.

The true criterion for a speed limit is – can I stop safely in the distance I can see to be safe?

Road conditions, weather conditions, vehicle condition, and driver condition all affect the maximum speed at which you should drive.

Allow other vehicles to get past you if they are breaking the speed limit: someone else will stop them soon enough.

Adjust your speed on the straight parts of the road, not on bends.

Q   What is a safe driving speed?

A   A speed inside the current speed limit at which you can still stop safely in the distance you can see to be safe.

Q   If I am driving at 30 mph in a built-up area and everyone else is going at speeds up to 50 or 60 mph, should I join them?

A   No, stick to the speed limits which you can see and you know are safe and legal.

Q   How do speed cameras work?

A   They are fitted at known locations and are triggered by vehicles passing them at higher than a preset speed. Camera images are now accepted in court as full and total evidence.

Q   Are speed cameras working all the time?

A   No, there are usually about ten cameras for every fifty or so sites, but you never know which ones are operating so you have to assume that each one is working and ready to take pictures at any time.

Q   On which side of the road should I drive when in a one-way street?

A   You should drive on the side of the road which will lead to your next turning. If there is no turning needed or expected, stay on the left unless you are overtaking.

Q   Are there any special dangers to look for in or near one-way streets?

A   Not dangers as such, but you do need to be extra careful when crossing them, or turning into them. Look out for traffic on what could be thought of as the wrong side.

Q   Does it matter what position I take up when turning right from a one-way street?

A   Yes, make sure you are in the right-hand lane, unless signs tell you otherwise.

Q   Can I turn into the right-hand lane of a one-way street?

A   Yes, if it is your intention to stay in the right-hand lane.

Q   If route directions are painted on the lanes, must I keep to them?

A   Yes, painted directions are road signs and need to be observed and followed.

Q   What should I do if I find that I am in the wrong lane going round a large gyratory one-way system?

A   If you are in the wrong lane you should go the way your lane dictates. Only change from that lane if it is absolutely safe.

Q   Which way should I look when going round gyratory one-way systems?

A   Look all round. Look over both shoulders to make sure you are not being overtaken.

Q   What signals should I use when using one-way gyratory systems and large roundabouts?

A   Signal your intention to change into any new lane, and signal before changing lanes as you drive round them. Finally you may have to signal left at the exit before you leave.

Q   If a direction lane is signed throughout a one-way gyratory system need I signal at all once I am in it?

A   If the lanes are signed throughout you may have to signal a lane change at the start, but once you are in that lane you may follow the lane throughout and leave without signalling.

Q   What are the basic shapes and meanings of road and traffic signs?

A   Circles must be obeyed, triangles warn, and rectangles inform.

Q   Do the colours of circular signs make any difference?

A   Red circles say what you must not do, and blue circles say what you must do.

Q   Why do some red circles have one or two red lines across them?

A   Red circles are mostly prohibitory, but some have a bar or a cross across the centre in order to emphasize the precise act which is prohibited.

Q   What colour and shape are warning signs?

A   Warning signs are red triangles.

Q   Are all triangular signs warnings?

A   Yes. The one possible exception is the upside-down triangle, but that actually warns you that a stop or give way sign is immediately ahead.

Q   What colour are local direction signs?

A   Local direction signs are usually black on white with a black border; local interest signs are usually white on brown with white borders.

Q   What colour are most motorway signs?

A   Most motorway signs are blue; the exceptions are the matrix signs overhead or on the central observations. These are usually made of separate lights which give different messages.

Q   Some rectangular signs are blue – why is this?

A   Most blue rectangles give positive instructions.

Q   Why are blue rectangular signs used on motorways?

A   These give information, directions, and positive instructions.

Q   What are green rectangular signs used for?

A   These are usually signs on primary routes – on main roads that are not motorways.

Q   There are a number of unusual signs consisting of yellow squares or rectangles with shapes – black circles, diamonds, and triangles in them. What are they for?

A   These are symbols used for emergency and long-term diversion signs. They are often used for motorway traffic as a help to get to airports or around large towns.

The Learner Driver Theory Test Paper 2

Thirty-five Questions on the Theoretical Training Syllabus for Learner Drivers

Choose the answers nearest to the options given which you think are correct; check your score against the answers shown on the answer page and then work out your score. The minimum acceptable score is 26 but before you consider yourself really ready to take the practical driving test you should score at least 32 out of 35.

Where more than one answer is needed, all must be correct to count.

Marks scored **/35**

Allow forty minutes for this test. Answer without using any books or assistance.

1 Drivers should never drink and drive, but what is the maximum level of alcohol which is allowed in a driver's breath before a mandatory driving ban would be imposed?

A   35 microgrammes of alcohol per 100 millilitres of breath.

B   55 microgrammes of alcohol per 100 millilitres of breath.

C   80 microgrammes of alcohol per 100 millilitres of breath.
D   107 microgrammes of alcohol per 100 millilitres of breath.

A ( )   B ( )   C ( )   D ( )

2   When travelling at 70 mph on a relatively empty three-lane rural motorway which lane should a driver normally choose to be in?
A   The nearside lane – lane one.
B   The middle lane – lane two.
C   The outside lane – lane three.
D   Any lane provided there is no one overtaking.

A ( )   B ( )   C ( )   D ( )

3   Which of the following actions must you *not* do before you leave your motor vehicle parked at the kerbside at a parking meter?
A   Apply the handbrake and switch off the engine.
B   Check that the sidelights are off.
C   Leave your headlights on dipped beam.
D   Switch on any alarm system.

A ( )   B ( )   C ( )   D ( )

4   All motor cars first registered more than three years ago are required to pass an MOT vehicle inspection. Which of the following would *not* result in failure of this test?
A   A cracked windscreen in front of the driver's seat.
B   A non-standard fuel cap.
C   A non-standard number plate.
D   No spare wheel or tyre available.

A ( )   B ( )   C ( )   D ( )

5   What is the minimum total stopping distance for a motor car travelling at 40 mph on a dry road in good conditions?
A   18 metres (59 feet).
B   24 metres (79 feet).
C   36 metres (118 feet).
D   53 metres (174 feet).

A ( )   B ( )   C ( )   D ( )

6   What are the TWO conditions a driver must satisfy before supervising a learner driver in a motor car?
A   Has passed a category B driving test this year.
B   Has a new, signed category B licence.
C   Has held a category B licence for three years.
D   Is at least twenty-one years of age.

A ( )   B ( )   C ( )   D ( )

7   What does the flashing amber light at a pelican crossing mean?
A   Drivers must give way to pedestrians on the pavement.
B   Drivers must give way to pedestrians who are crossing.
C   Drivers must wait for the lights to turn red.
D   Drivers must wait for the lights to turn green.

A ( )   B ( )   C ( )   D ( )

8   In which of the following circumstances would you definitely *not* be required to apply your handbrake?
A   At traffic lights when the lights are red.
B   When stopping the car in an emergency.
C   When leaving the car parked on a hill in gear.
D   When leaving the car parked in your own garage.

A ( )   B ( )   C ( )   D ( )

9   You are approaching a long left-hand bend on a country lane in a national speed limit area. What should you do?
A   Move out to cross the centre line.
B   Move as close to the verge as possible.
C   Brake hard and select second gear.
D   Maintain the same distance from the verge.

A ( )   B ( )   C ( )   D ( )

10   Signals should be used to warn other road users of your intentions. Before which of the following would you *always* give a signal?
A   Moving off from the kerbside.
B   Turning left or right at a crossroads.

C   Moving off from behind a parked car.
D   Stopping at the kerbside.

A ( )   B ( )   C ( )   D ( )

11   Turning the car in the road is an exercise carried out during the driving test. In which of the following day-to-day driving activities would you find it best to do this manoeuvre?
A   After finding you have overshot your exit on a motorway.
B   When you need to turn back on a dual carriageway.
C   When driving down a one-way street.
D   When turning round in a wide quiet residential street.

A ( )   B ( )   C ( )   D ( )

12   At a narrow crossroads with traffic lights you wish to turn right. Facing you is a motor cycle, which is also signalling to turn right. When the lights go green which of the following is the *safest* procedure to follow?
A   Wait for the motor cyclist to disappear.
B   Wave to the motor cyclist, telling him to cross in front of you.
C   Move forward slowly, making eye contact with the rider.
D   Drive quickly to the middle of the road and take up your position.

A ( )   B ( )   C ( )   D ( )

13   Which of the following traffic light colours or combination of colours does *not* mean stop?
A   Green and amber.
B   Red and amber.
C   Amber on its own.
D   A green filter arrow.

A ( )   B ( )   C ( )   D ( )

14   Which of the following statements about traffic accidents is most likely *not* to be true?
A   Children are less at risk than adult pedestrians.
B   Most pedestrian accidents occur within 100 metres (109 yards) of crossings.

C   Road accidents are 25% to blame for all child deaths.
D   Drivers and riders are solely responsible for 85% of road deaths.

A ( )   B ( )   C ( )   D ( )

15   You are driving at about 30 mph along a quiet winding country lane when you come across a herd of cows walking slowly towards you, but occupying the whole of the road and verges. What should you do?
A   Sound your horn at intervals and keep going.
B   Stop immediately and check your mirrors.
C   Take the crown of the road and keep going.
D   Check your mirrors and slow down or stop.

A ( )   B ( )   C ( )   D ( )

16   You are driving in a four-lane city road when the car ahead slows down for a pedestrian crossing. There is no one crossing but two children are at the edge of the pavement apparently waiting to cross. What must you *not* do?
A   Wait behind the car ahead for the children to cross.
B   Check your mirrors, give an arm signal, and slow down to stop.
C   Overtake the car and drive on before the children move.
D   Stop your car alongside the leading car.

A ( )   B ( )   C ( )   D ( )

17   You are parking your car at night in a built-up area with street lights. Which of the following would be illegal?
A   Parking on the wrong side of the road.
B   Parking 15 metres (49 feet) from a junction.
C   Parking without side- or parking lights.
D   Parking on a single yellow line.

A ( )   B ( )   C ( )   D ( )

18   You are driving to work at 25 mph in a long line of traffic early in the morning. It has been raining heavily all night, but it is clearing up now. What distance is the minimum gap you should allow from the vehicle ahead?

A   Leave enough room for a motor cyclist to pull in.
B   One foot for every mile per hour – 8 metres (25 feet).
C   One metre for every mile per hour – 25 metres (82 feet).
D   Fourteen car lengths – 55 metres (180 feet).

A ( )   B ( )   C ( )   D ( )

19   You are approaching a pedestrian crossing in driving rain. On the pavement on the opposite side of the road you see an elderly couple; the man is using a white stick. They are apparently waiting to cross the road. What can you do best to assist them?
A   Flash your lights to oncoming traffic to stop.
B   Stop your car and wait for them to cross.
C   Drive on and hope they will get across on their own.
D   Drive past them, park safely, and walk back to help.

A ( )   B ( )   C ( )   D ( )

20   Which of the following is an illegal use of the horn?
A   Sounding it when seeing children playing.
B   Sounding it at midnight in the country.
C   Sounding it at 7.15 in the morning in town.
D   Sounding it whilst stationary to call a friend.

A ( )   B ( )   C ( )   D ( )

21   What speed limit is imposed on a learner driver who is driving on single carriageways where the national speed limit is in force?
A   30 mph.
B   40 mph.
C   50 mph.
D   60 mph.

A ( )   B ( )   C ( )   D ( )

22   You are driving along a busy rural motorway when you notice your steering seems heavy and you discover you have a puncture in your front offside tyre. What should you do?
A   Pull on to the hard shoulder and call the police.
B   Use the central reservation as cover whilst you change the wheel.

C   Drive on to the next motorway service station for assistance.
D   Pull on to the hard shoulder and change the wheel yourself.

A ( )   B ( )   C ( )   D ( )

23   What is the national speed limit for a dual-carriageway road?
A   50 mph.
B   55 mph.
C   60 mph.
D   70 mph.

A ( )   B ( )   C ( )   D ( )

24   You are driving in a small market town and intend to turn
left into a turning 100 metres (109 yards) up the road. Ahead of
you a large rigid furniture lorry is signalling left, but as it gets
closer to the turning it swings out to the right. What should you
do?
A   Move on the inside in order to make your turning now.
B   Sound your horn to remind him that he is signalling wrongly.
C   Drop back so that you can be seen in his mirrors.
D   Close the gap to make good progress.

A ( )   B ( )   C ( )   D ( )

25   Shapes and colours are used to indicate different types of road
sign. The purpose of a red triangle generally indicates which of the
following?
A   Warning sign.
B   Prohibitory sign.
C   Mandatory sign.
D   Information sign.

A ( )   B ( )   C ( )   D ( )

26   Signals given by drivers to police officers and other authorized
persons should be clear and distinct. If your intention is to go
straight ahead what signal would you give a police officer in front
of you?
A   Your left hand facing the windscreen.
B   Your right hand facing the windscreen.

C   Your right arm out of the window palm upwards.
D   Your left arm across the windscreen.

A ( )   B ( )   C ( )   D ( )

27   You have just bought your first motor car and have been given the registration document by the person selling it to you. What legal actions are now required to be carried out with regard to this document?
A   You do nothing, but the seller sends it off to DVLA.
B   Both you and the seller sign the document and you each send off your part.
C   You alone have to fill in the changed details and send them to DVLA.
D   You need do nothing until the tax disc needs renewing.

A ( )   B ( )   C ( )   D ( )

28   Which TWO of the following will prevent you from being allowed to learn to drive?
A   You are a registered diabetic and must take insulin treatment.
B   You are profoundly deaf and cannot use a hearing aid.
C   You cannot read a number plate at 20.5 metres (67 feet).
D   You have had a daytime epileptic seizure this year.

A ( )   B ( )   C ( )   D ( )

29   You are involved in a motor-car accident with a motor cycle. There are some injuries to the motor cyclist, but you are not sure how serious. Which TWO of the following should you do as soon as possible?
A   Get someone to call the emergency services.
B   Remove the motor cyclist's helmet and loosen their clothing.
C   Switch off all engines and impose a smoking ban.
D   Move the motor cyclist off the road on to the pavement.

A ( )   B ( )   C ( )   D ( )

30   You have a breakdown on a motorway and your vehicle is moved to the hard shoulder for a motoring organization to work on it. At what distance from the vehicle should you place a red warning triangle?

A   25 metres (82 feet).
B   50 metres (164 feet).
C   100 metres (109 yards).
D   150 metres (164 yards).

A ( )   B ( )   C ( )   D ( )

31 Some road markings are used to indicate that parking or waiting is not allowed on that stretch of road. In which of the following would parking be permitted in some circumstances?
A   The zigzag marking approaching a zebra crossing.
B   Where double white lines are painted in the centre of the road.
C   Where three yellow bars are painted across the edge of the road.
D   Where a single yellow line is painted along the edge of the road.

A ( )   B ( )   C ( )   D ( )

32 You are driving along at 70 mph in lane two of a three-lane rural motorway with traffic in both lanes alongside you. Up ahead you see a lorry jack-knife across the carriageway and you need to stop in an emergency. Which of the following would you *not* do?
A   Check your mirrors and brake gently then progressively to stop.
B   Hit the footbrake as hard as you can, holding the steering-wheel firmly.
C   Switch your hazard lights on and brake firmly.
D   Move quickly across to the hard shoulder.

A ( )   B ( )   C ( )   D ( )

33 You are approaching a set of traffic lights in a 50 mph speed limit. They are showing green and you are still about 200 metres (218 yards) away. Your speed is 40 mph and there are four vehicles between you and the traffic lights. What should you do?
A   Brake now and slow down to get to the lights at green again.
B   Keep going until the lights change to red and then brake to stop.
C   Accelerate to 50 mph to beat the traffic lights changing.
D   Check your mirrors, adjust your speed, and plan to stop.

A ( )   B ( )   C ( )   D ( )

34 You are learning to drive and need some practice in addition to your driving lessons. Which TWO of the following would be illegal?

A   To pay a friend to cover their petrol costs.
B   To get some practice in your family car.
C   To take lessons from a friend who passed their test last year.
D   To let a friend give you lessons in a van without windows.

A ( )   B ( )   C ( )   D ( )

35 You have recently bought your own car, which is four years old. Which THREE of the following vehicle checks should you carry out each week?

A   Check your tyre tread, depth and pressures.
B   Clean windscreens, windows, and lights.
C   Check brake, clutch, and other fluid levels.
D   Check the exhaust emissions for legal levels.

A ( )   B ( )   C ( )   D ( )

The Learner Driver Theory Test – Answer Sheet Paper 2

1		2		3		4		5	
A	X	A	X	A	☐	A	☐	A	☐
B	☐	B	☐	B	☐	B	☐	B	☐
C	☐	C	☐	C	X	C	☐	C	X
D	☐	D	☐	D	☐	D	X	D	☐

6		7		8		9		10	
A	☐	A	☐	A	☐	A	☐	A	☐
B	☐	B	X	B	X	B	☐	B	X
C	X	C	☐	C	☐	C	☐	C	☐
D	X	D	☐	D	☐	D	X	D	☐

11		12		13		14		15	
A	☐	A	☐	A	☐	A	X	A	☐
B	☐	B	☐	B	☐	B	☐	B	☐
C	☐	C	X	C	☐	C	☐	C	☐
D	X	D	☐	D	X	D	☐	D	X

16		17		18		19		20	
A	☐	A	☐	A	☐	A	☐	A	☐
B	☐	B	X	B	☐	B	X	B	☐
C	X	C	☐	C	X	C	☐	C	☐
D	☐	D	☐	D	☐	D	☐	D	X

21		22		23		24		25	
A	☐	A	X	A	☐	A	☐	A	X
B	☐	B	☐	B	☐	B	☐	B	☐
C	☐	C	☐	C	☐	C	X	C	☐
D	X	D	☐	D	X	D	☐	D	☐

26		27		28		29		30	
A	X	A	☐	A	☐	A	X	A	☐
B	☐	B	X	B	☐	B	☐	B	☐
C	☐	C	☐	C	X	C	X	C	☐
D	☐	D	☐	D	X	D	☐	D	X

31		32		33		34		35	
A	☐	A	☐	A	☐	A	X	A	X
B	☐	B	☐	B	☐	B	☐	B	X
C	☐	C	X	C	☐	C	X	C	X
D	X	D	☐	D	X	D	☐	D	☐

Safe Driving for Life

1. Driving as a skill

Once the main manipulative skills of vehicle handling have been mastered, many drivers think they have learned it all. They soon find that this is not so, and what has still to be learned is much more important; in some ways, it can be more difficult to assimilate. They now have to improve their perception and information-processing skills to a stage where they can be trusted to get on with the serious aspects of driving on autopilot. Once they can carry out the mechanical driving tasks without conscious thought, they can get on with the mental processes of driving. These are the real driving skills.

After a reasonable amount of practice, learner drivers gain more confidence and skill, and their instructors will be able to trust them to get on with the practical aspects of changing gear, steering, accelerating, and braking. The instructor will then direct the learner to give more attention to the real driving task. This is achieved by scanning the road ahead for anything which will require a change of speed or direction.

What learners now need to learn is recognition, identification, and decision-making skills with regard to potential hazards. The real problem that faces learner drivers at this stage is that they are presented with so much detail ahead and around that they need to be taught how to filter out less important information. All of this has to be carried out in the time that the vehicle is driving towards the problem with the decision an irrevocable one. It is this time factor in hazard perception which requires the assistance of a good professional and skilled instructor. A good instructor will give tips on the recognition of hazards and guide the learner to make correct reactions to hazard potential.

FACT FILE

Driving is a complex task which consists of a variety of skills which combine together and are supported by a whole range of background knowledge and previous experience.

Hazard recognition, identification, and planning needs careful teaching.

Visual search and scanning systems can be made easier by listening to good commentary-style driving from a professional instructor.

New drivers need to hone their observation skills and combine them with the speed of their reactions in order to react correctly and promptly to each new hazard.

Hazard perception follows a pattern of looking ahead, seeing what is important, observing that which will need action, and perceiving the correct action to be taken.

Hazards are not just junctions, traffic lights, people, other vehicles, and zebra crossings: they include such things as changes to the road surface, raised drains which cause cyclists to swerve, a low sun shining into the windscreen, smeared windscreens and failing to make eye contact with oncoming road users.

Q Why is it so difficult for new drivers to look far enough ahead?

A New drivers normally only travel at walking pace and do not project themselves far enough forward.

Q How far ahead should a driver be looking?

A It is difficult to give a fixed distance, but in terms of seconds' travel, you must look at least five to ten seconds ahead of you. You need to be planning for fifteen to twenty seconds if you can.

Q How far can I travel in five seconds?

A At 30 mph you will cover 68 metres (223 feet).

Q How far would I travel in ten seconds at 70 mph?

A 318 metres (347 yards) or one fifth of a mile.

Q Am I expected to notice and inspect everything that is in front of you in that distance?

A No, that would be impossible, which is why you need to be selective in what you see. This is what proper visual search techniques are all about.

Q How do I select what to look at and what to ignore?

A You must look for anything in the distance which may cause you to change speed or position. Then you must decide whether to start slowing down now, or to keep at the same speed but making allowances for it.

Q Can you give me an example of how this visual search technique works?

A Yes. Imagine you are driving at 60 mph on a single carriageway. In the distance you can see a set of traffic lights. They are green now and you have to estimate how long it will take you to reach them, and how you can get there when they are green again.

Q Do visual search techniques mean that you have to take some form of action for everything you see?

A You have to consider everything. It may be a Sunday and you see a school warning ahead. If you then search around and realize that the school is closed, and there are no children around, you can safely ignore that particular warning.

Q But does it mean I have to think about everything you see?

A Yes; you have to make a conscious or subconscious decision to act on or ignore any potential for change. The real skill of driving is making correct decisions.

Q Does that mean I have to make an instant and permanent decision to slow down or not?

A No, it means you continue to make and adjust your decisions all the time you are approaching and thinking about coping with the potential hazard ahead.

Q How often should I brake and change gear for each hazard you see?

A You would normally make one braking decision and one gear-change decision for each hazard you encounter.

Q Is a single set of traffic lights 100 metres (109 yards) up the road a simple hazard?

A Not necessarily. A single set of traffic lights up ahead could be broken down into a number of separate stages; therefore each one stage could need a single acceleration or braking action, followed by a separate gear change for each one.

Q How can I best prepare myself for this stage of my driver training?

A Once you have reached a reasonable stage of vehicle-handling competence you need to practise thinking about your driving and making all your own decisions on what you will be doing in five seconds' time.

Q Why is five seconds such a critical time factor in driving?

A You will know about the two-second rule. That only applies to a good driver in a good vehicle with good tyres and on a good road surface. Anything which is not perfect adds extra time. A learner driver needs at least five seconds' safety time for seeing, thinking, and acting.

Q Is five seconds the furthest ahead I need to look when I am driving?

A No, five seconds is the minimum distance. The further ahead you see and make decisions the better the driver you will become.

Q How does the two-second rule actually work?

A If you are closer than two seconds to the vehicle in front then you are much too close and in danger of running into the back of them.

Q How do I carry out a two-second or five-second following-distance check?

A Watch out for a mark or post on the road ahead. Count the time from when the vehicle in front passes it until you reach it. You must have at least five seconds' safety gap to be confident of stopping.

Q Does that mean that most drivers on the road are unsafe? They all seem to drive much closer than that.

A Yes, unfortunately most drivers follow the vehicle ahead much too closely, but because they get away with it most times, they assume they will always get away with it. They don't, and this is the cause of most road-traffic accidents.

Q What happens when the vehicle ahead brakes?

A Provided the braking is gentle and planned, all the vehicles behind manage to stop as well. But if the braking is hurried or unexpected, some of the following vehicles will collide.

Q What is the greatest single cause of vehicle collisions?

A   Driving too close to the vehicle in front, and driving in a queue of traffic all following too close to each other.

Q   Do observation and hazard perception skills improve with age and experience?

A   They can do, but only if drivers make a conscious effort to train themselves in the skill. Too many drivers never bother and never learn from experience either.

Q   What can I do to make myself a safer driver?

A   Practise your visual search skills all the time, not just when you are learning to drive, but when you have passed your test too.

Q   What are the benefits of using perceptive skills in driving?

A   If you train and practise your perceptive skills you will always avoid being involved in other people's incidents and drive safely for a long time to come.

2. Other factors which affect your vehicle-handling skills

You must realize that many things affect the way you drive and the way you cope with the driving conditions you will meet. Your own reaction times will vary from day to day, and will certainly deteriorate very badly when you are tired or not feeling well. But the speed at which you react is only one factor in coping with various road and traffic hazards.

Your vehicle's stability will be noticeably affected by the way you load it – either with passengers or goods. If there are four or five large adults in a small Fiesta-size saloon car it will take much longer to brake, and will not hold the road on bends as well as it will when you are driving alone. If you load a pile of heavy bricks or suitcases into the boot of an estate car the effect on the braking and steering will be quite dramatic. The weight transfer is wrong, and you cannot steer properly if the boot takes all the weight.

Apart from the various legal restrictions, common sense must also play a large part. Drivers on their way home from the local DIY store with long poles stuck out of the front passenger's windows are a bit reminiscent of knights in armour with lances at full tilt. The result when they hit a passing cyclist is quite frightening too.

FACT FILE

Loading needs thinking through; make sure everything is secure. Heavy loads in the back seriously affect steering.

You should never carry more passengers than you have seats for.

Do not allow children to sit on their parents' laps.

Only carry children if you have suitable restraints or booster cushions.

Your vehicle handbook will state the maximum loads you should carry.

Do not allow long loads to project outside your vehicle.

Q What are the dangers of driving an overloaded car?

A You lose a lot of steering control and your brakes are not so effective.

Q Are there any additional dangers from having too many passengers in the back?

A Yes; apart from any distractions, the added weight will make handling difficult.

Q What is the 'flying granny' syndrome?

A This is a term given to the effect of an unbelted rear-seat passenger flying forward in the event of harsh braking. It can cause serious injury to the front-seat passengers in an emergency.

Q Is this why it is dangerous for children to stand between the front seats?

A Yes, not only is it illegal, it is stupid and thoughtless.

Q Are learner drivers allowed to tow caravans or trailers?

A No. Only full category B licence holders can tow caravans or trailers.

Q Can new drivers tow caravans or trailers when they get their full category B licence?

A No. Anyone who passes their driving test after 1st July 1996 must take a separate driving test before being allowed to tow a large caravan or trailer.

Q   What is the maximum sized trailer that can be towed by a new full category B licence holder?
A   Their maximum towing weight is 750 kilogrammes (15 hundred-weight). This is smaller than most caravans.
Q   What should I do if I am asked to tow another vehicle?
A   If your licence allows you to tow, check that the tow-rope fixings are secure and arrange a code of signals between you and the driver being towed.
Q   What should I do if I need to be towed by someone else?
A   Check the two-rope fixings and arrange signals as above. Keep the tow rope relatively taut when being pulled; don't allow it to become slack, or get too close to the towing vehicle.
Q   Is there a maximum length of tow rope?
A   Yes, 4.5 metres (15 feet).
Q   Are there any other restrictions on tow ropes?
A   Yes, if the length is more than 1.5 metres (5 feet) make sure there is a flag or other visual sign in the middle of the rope.
Q   Should I accept a tow if my brakes have failed?
A   No, unless you are being towed by a vehicle using a rigid tow-bar.

3. Driving in difficult conditions

Normal driving conditions cover a whole range of activities, but every learner driver and new driver needs preparation for the additional problems – or perhaps they could be called 'challenges' – which arise in more difficult conditions. These include driving at night, driving in bad weather, and driving on motorways. Learner drivers are not allowed to drive in cars or on motor cycles on motorways, but good professional instructors will always ensure that their pupils gain plenty of useful practice on local dual carriageways constructed to motorway standards. If learners cannot get this practice, they can still take a long-distance lesson after the test which will incorporate motorway skills.

Driving at night brings immediate limitations of visibility. This applies not only to you seeing other road users and identifying potential hazards in the dark, but also to ensuring that your own vehicle is fully visible to anyone on the road who might need to be aware of your presence, intentions, size, and speed. Headlights should be used whenever visibility drops below 100 metres, or when you find it difficult to see ahead. Your headlights are used not only to help you to see other road users and street furniture, but to make sure that other people can see and recognize you as a motor vehicle.

When it's dark you should use your headlights, either dipped or main beam, depending upon the ambient lighting conditions at the time. Parking lights are for parking only, and sidelights are almost useless at night. Some vehicles are fitted with an in-between style of light, called 'dim-dip' and this provides adequate lighting for the vehicle to be outlined when the street lighting is good, but they are not good enough to see with in the dark.

FACT FILE

Headlights should be used whenever visibility falls below 100 metres (109 yards).

Dipped headlights should be used when following or approaching other traffic at night.

Lights must be in working order, even during daylight.

Headlights or front fog lights must be used when visibility drops below 100 metres in daylight.

Low-slung front fog lights must not be used except in fog or falling snow.

Rear fog lights can be used at night when visibility is bad.

All fog lights must be turned off when not needed.

Be prepared to slow down or stop if oncoming vehicle lights dazzle you.

Flashing headlights only have one meaning: to say you are there.

Q   During what times should you put on your headlights?
A   From half an hour after sunset until half an hour before sunrise.
Q   What is the meaning of a headlight flash?
A   To draw attention to someone's presence on the road.
Q   When can you use hazard-warning lights whilst stationary?

A   Only when the vehicle is stopped to warn of a temporary obstruction.

Q   When can I use vehicle hazard-warning lights whilst I am moving?

A   Only on motorways or dual carriageways with 70 mph speed limits, and only then to warn of unusual hazards or obstructions ahead.

Q   How do I know if my headlights are not properly adjusted?

A   If others drivers flash at you, or you can get your garage to test them for you. Headlights can be altered by carrying extra weight in the boot.

Q   Can I use dipped headlights in the dark in a built-up area?

A   Yes, you would normally just use dipped lights in towns. Main beams would dazzle people.

Q   How can I cut down glare at night in town driving?

A   You can drive on dim-dipped lights if your vehicle is fitted with them.

Q   If I am on main beam at night in the country when taking bends, do I need to dip my lights at the same time to turn right and to turn left?

A   No. Sometimes you can hold on to your main-beam lights longer when taking right-hand bends. Watch where they are pointing and make sure that you don't dazzle other road users.

Q   When parking at night should I leave my vehicle lights on?

A   You can leave sidelights or parking lights on; but you must not leave headlights switched on whether dipped or main beam.

4. Driving in bad weather conditions

Bad weather conditions are probably fairly normal in our British climate, and in some ways most learner drivers are lucky because in the three to six months that many take to master the practical skills of driving they can reckon to have seen most types of weather, from bright sunshine to heavy downpours of rain.

The first thing to remember is that in any form of bad weather driving your tyres will not grip the road surfaces as well and therefore you need to drive more slowly, and to allow more time for stopping.

In rain it is more difficult to see and to be seen. Sensible vehicle lights need to be switched on. In some driving conditions where visibility is poor you will notice how easily you can see vehicles showing rear fog lights and how difficult it is to see those using normal rear lights. Use this clue to tell you when to use your own high-intensity rear fog lights. However you must not use low-slung front fog lights, except in falling snow or thick fog. Switch off all these extra lights as soon as conditions improve.

Snow, ice, and fog all bring additional problems and challenges to drivers. This is especially so when you are confronted with them for the first time. If you learn to drive and pass your test during the summer months it is always a good thing to go back to your professional driving instructor for a few extra lessons when the weather is bad. The best way to cope with driving in bad weather is to take good professional intelligent instruction.

FACT FILE

Before starting any journey in bad weather conditions check or do the following;

Tyre pressures are correct, and the tread depth is more than adequate.

Clear all snow, ice, or dirt from windows and windscreens.

Top up the washer bottle, and check the wiper blades.

Consider putting pieces of old sacking in the boot if snow is expected.

Have warm clothing or old blanket in the car in case you get stuck anywhere.

Tell someone where you are going, and let them know when you arrive.

When driving in snow and ice:

When starting or driving on snow or ice use minimum acceleration.

Start in a higher gear and avoid sudden movements.

Avoid wheelspin especially when starting or changing gear.

Allow enormous distances between you and vehicles ahead.

Never drive any faster than you really know you can stop in.

Q   In foggy weather should I use my headlights on main-beam?

A   Don't use main-beam lights as they will dazzle you as well.

Q   Should I use dipped lights in thick fog?

A   Yes, dipped lights will give you the best view of the road. Use fog lights too if you have them fitted, and if no one is very close behind use rear fog lights as well.

Q   How closely should I follow other traffic when I am driving in fog?

A   Avoid getting closer than your braking distance allows. Keep your speed down so that you can always stop safely in the distance you can see ahead.

Q   If the vehicle ahead of me is going too slowly in fog, should I overtake?

A   No. It is much easier to follow someone in fog than to be first in the queue.

Q   Why is it easier to follow someone in foggy weather?

A   Because the leading vehicle disturbs the fog and mist. You can also see and take advantage of their lights ahead of you.

Q   Are there any additional tips I can remember to use in foggy conditions?

A   Yes; clean your windows regularly, especially inside. Don't have your own private fog inside the car.

Q   Why is driving on ice dangerous?

A   Because your stopping distances are enormous. It takes up to ten times more to stop on ice. If the ice is really bad and you pick up speed, the only thing that might stop you is another vehicle or piece of street furniture.

Q   At what speed should I drive when the roads are icy?

A   No faster than a walking pace, unless you are really sure you can still stop safely.

Q   What additional problems are then when driving on ice?

A   First of all — other traffic. Try not to get too close to other vehicles. Try not to steer, brake, or accelerate excessively.

Q   Should I use my screen-washers in the winter?

A   You may get your windscreen frozen over if you use a screen-washer fluid that is not effective. This can seriously reduce your visibility. Use proper de-icer liquid in your washer bottle.

Q   Can I use anti-freeze in my windscreen-washer bottle?

A   No, definitely not. Anti-freeze will damage your car's paintwork.

Q   How should I drive in snow?

A   With the greatest possible care. Try to keep your tyres in any previous tracks made by other vehicles if you can. Keep your speed down so that you can always stop safely in the distance you can see to be safe.

Q   What should I do if I have to drive on virgin snow?

A   Try to see or work out what is underneath the snow. Avoid driving across genuinely unknown surfaces. You could easily go off the road, into deep water or even a ditch.

Q   What additional problems do I face when driving in falling snow?

A   Lack of visibility for yourself and for other road users. Clean your windows, regularly, but try to avoid stopping where it may be difficult to start again.

Q   Should I use my windscreen wipers in falling snow?

A   Yes, you may need to keep them going all the time. Keep your rear window clear too. Avoid a build-up of snow on the windows or headlights.

Q   Does starting a car in snow present difficulties?

A   Each time you stop and start or change direction you may have a problem starting again. Avoid stopping on hills, steep cambers, or where you can see frozen snow or ice.

Q   What advice can you give about riding a motor cycle in snow or ice?

A   Don't.

Q   What are the problems with driving in heavy rain?

A   Poor visibility and increased braking distances are two problems. You will find it more difficult to see, and others may not see you easily either. Braking distances are more than doubled on wet roads, and if the rain is very heavy even good tyres cannot always shift the water through the treads. The wipers may not clear the water off the screen effectively.

Q   What is the best position on the road to drive in heavy rain?

A   Try to stay on the crown of the road if you can. This is where the water is normally at its most shallow.

Q   Are my brakes effective after I have driven through a flood?

A   No. Dry your brakes gently keeping your left foot on the brake pedal for about five seconds or so, to get rid of excess water. Try your brakes to be sure.

Q   Are there any extra difficulties I might face when driving in the rain?

A   Think about cyclists and pedestrians. Not only are they getting wetter than you are, you can easily splash them if you are not careful.

Q   Are there any special things I should remember about driving in high winds?

A   Yes, it is not so much the effect that strong winds can have directly on you; but you must be extra careful when overtaking high-sided vehicles or driving through cuttings. Be prepared for sudden additional high pressure as you clear the obstruction.

Q   Are caravans more at risk in high winds?

A   Yes, but this doesn't only mean to take care when towing one yourself, look out for additional risks when you follow or approach a vehicle towing a caravan or trailer.

Q   Learner drivers are not allowed to tow caravans; should they take extra training after their driving test?

A   Certainly, and you will need additional training in all weather conditions.

Q   Is sunshine the best weather condition of all to drive in?

A   Not always. A low sun in the winter, or early mornings and late evenings can easily blind you.

Q   Is it all right when the sun is behind me, then?

A   No. You need to remember that any oncoming traffic may be blinded instead.

Q   What are the general rules for bad weather driving?

A   Always keep a safety cushion around you when you drive, and if any of the conditions which exist make life difficult, give yourself double, treble, or even ten times as much time and room.

5. You will also need to know about the practical driving test

The driving test has been with us for over sixty years now, and the written theory is the greatest single change in that time. It does mean that you will be better prepared for the test. By the time you have studied all the background material, you will find that most of the knowledge you have acquired, and the attitudes you have developed, will make the practical test much easier.

For the first six months you will be able to take the two tests in either order; but from 1st January 1997 you will need to have a pass certificate from the theory test in order to take the practical one.

FACT FILE

Driving examiners are not looking for great skill or experience, but for competence.

Competence can be defined as having the potential to continue learning in safety.

Vehicles must be provided by the candidate, and must be roadworthy.

They do not have to be driving-school cars, nor fitted with dual controls.

Candidates for test must know, and have to state, that the vehicle is properly insured.

Candidates are required to carry out a series of prescribed exercises around pre-set test routes.

The practical test is not an ordeal. If you know how to control the car, you can think for yourself, and you can convince the examiner that you will be able to carry on learning on your own, safely, afterwards, you will pass.

Q Can I take the practical test at any test centre I choose?

A Yes, you can select any test centre anywhere in the country.

Q Are the test centres the same for theory and practical tests?

A No, they are quite different types of tests, needing totally different testing procedures.

Q Do I need a driving licence to take both tests?

A Yes, you must hold a proper provisional and signed driving licence for both tests.

Q Will the examiner know how many times I have taken the test?

A Driving examiners try not to discover anything about you, except what you demonstrate to them.

Q How do driving examiners actually mark down any faults when I am on test?

A Every action you take is looked at to see if you do it safely. Their method of marking is to grade all the mistakes you make into four different kinds.

Q What are the four separate grades of error which an examiner will notice about my driving?

A   Unrecorded errors; minor errors; serious errors; and dangerous errors.

Q   What sort of mistakes are regarded as unrecorded errors?

A   Most mistakes you make are regarded as insignificant. These
aren't recorded and are not considered worth discussing.

Q   But the examiner does mark some mistakes as minor, even
though they don't cause me to fail. What are they?

A   Minor errors do not actually involve any other road users; they
are marked down and discussed with you at the end of the test.

Q   Am I limited to how many minor mistakes I make before I fail?

A   No. You can make dozens and it still won't matter. But you will
be told about them after the test, and you will need to improve a
lot if you want to be a really good driver.

Q   What sort of mistakes will fail me, then?

A   The examiners decide if any errors you make are serious or
dangerous. Serious mistakes are the sort that could cause you
to have an accident if you continue to drive that way.

Q   What constitutes a dangerous mistake?

A   A dangerous mistake is one that causes another road user
actually to change direction or speed because of something the
candidate did during the drive.

Q   Can you give an example of an unrecorded error?

A   If you brake too hard when stopping, so that you do so with a jerk
instead of gently bringing the vehicle to rest, the examiner
would disregard this occasional mistake.

Q   Of a minor error?

A   If you approached an open right turn and cut the corner slightly
into a clear opening, this is an example of untidy driving. It
would not cause you to fail, but the examiner would need to
mention it to you afterwards.

Q   What is an example of a serious error?

A   If you cut the same right corner, turning into an open junction,
but there was a parked van on your right – even if no one was
coming up the road, you would not know, and this is a serious
error.

Q   What is an example of a dangerous error?

A   If you cut a right-hand corner and could not see it was safe, and
an oncoming vehicle was forced to brake to avoid you, this is a
dangerous error.

Q   If I make a dangerous error will the examiner take over control
from me, like my instructor would?

A Driving examiners are not normally allowed to take control of the car except where 'life and limb' are at risk. If they do intervene at all in the test, it is stopped at that point and you will already have failed.

Q What sort of intervention can an examiner do?

A They sometimes have to use their voice to take verbal control. Or they can actually take the steering, or apply the brakes if they have dual controls. This is physical intervention.

Q Do examiners have to take action very often on driving tests?

A Regrettably this happens much more than it should. About ten per cent of driving tests are aborted because the candidates are not safe.

Q How can I make sure that the examiner will not take action and abandon my driving test?

A You must have plenty of pre-test practice, and also allow your instructor to give you plenty of dummy tests during which he doesn't give any advice, instruction, or guidance.

Q How will I know if I am ready to pass the driving test?

A You must be able to drive – following simple route directions – without any help or comments from your instructor for at least five lessons before you take the test. That way you will know you are good enough to pass.

6. After the driving test: the motorway

Perhaps one of the best – or possibly the worst – feelings in the world of driving is when you actually get in the car with a full category B driving licence and drive off on your own. You have to make all your own decisions, and you alone choose where to go, what gear to do it in, and – this is the difficult bit – when and where you fill up with fuel.

Driving alone really is a wonderful feeling. This is what makes all the lessons, the studying, and the practice really worthwhile. But there are still lots of things to learn, and you must plan to continue to learn to drive even after the test. Most importantly, you need to know what sort of journeys you are going to make and how long each journey will last. You are no longer limited to one- or two-hour driving lessons or practice around town or near test routes. You will soon have to go on a motorway; this is real fun. The problem with motorways is that they mean totally different things to different people. Those who live in Cornwall or the Lake District know them to be super-highways which allow them to get away from little villages and twisting country roads. Those who live near the Aston Expressway in Birmingham, or in any dormitory town feeding on to the M25, will know that some motorways are more like permanent traffic jams. The M25 itself has been described as the world's largest roundabout and sometimes the world's largest car park. But like them or not, motorways are not only here to stay, they are lots safer than any other road you are ever likely to drive on, so get used to them.

FACT FILE

Driving on motorways

You normally join motorways from a slip-road on the left.

Give way to traffic already on the motorway and adjust your speed to suit

Join the left-hand lane and stay there until you need to overtake.

Take your time, stay in the left lane until you are used to the speed.

Keep exceptional lane discipline and stay centred in that lane.

Only change lanes when you really need to overtake slower traffic.

Get back into the left-hand lane when there is space and time.

Drive at a steady cruising speed well within your car's capabilities.

Don't drive at the maximum speed just for the fun of it.

Keep an even greater safety cushion around you than on slower roads.

Motorways can make you drowsy. Take plenty of breaks.

Never drive on the hard shoulder and only stop there if it is vital.

Look out for and obey all motorway signals. Some signs look different; learn all about them before going on a motorway.

> **Better still, have a few lessons with a profes-
> sional instructor.**
> **Leave motorways from the left lane (but not
> always – some roads in Glasgow and the
> M25/A21 Sevenoaks in Kent leave from the
> right!).**
> **Check your speed when you do leave – you
> may be faster than you think.**
> **Breakdowns on motorways have special
> rules; read all about them.**

Q   How do I know if I am approaching a motorway?

A   All motorways are specially signposted and an alternative route is shown.

Q   Can anyone drive on a motorway?

A   No; most learner drivers are specifically forbidden, so they must use the alternative routes.

Q   Why are motorways safer than ordinary roads?

A   Because they are straighter and have only shallow bends. There is no crossing or oncoming traffic, and you have more room to plan your driving and think.

Q   What speed limits apply to new drivers on motorways?

A   The same as for everyone else. Speed limits are fixed for roads and vehicles, and not for the drivers.

Q   What is the longest period of time I should drive on a motorway?

A   If this is your first time, or you are not used to motorway driving, an hour is ample.

Q   How long should experienced drivers stay at the wheel on motorways?

A   Two hours is enough for anyone. Even experienced drivers need breaks.

Q   What should I do if I feel sleepy on the motorway?

A   Don't nod off. Force yourself to keep awake, but slow down and concentrate until you get to the next exit. Then pull off the motorway and find somewhere to get out and walk around until you are completely revitalized.

Q   Is feeling sleepy on motorways the only danger?

A   No. Watch out for others who may feel sleepy – they could cause you trouble as well.

Q   What is the first thing I should do if I have a breakdown on the motorway?

A   Get off the motorway if you can. Try to reach the next exit or service station. They are rarely more than five or ten miles apart.

Q   What do I do if I have a breakdown and cannot reach the next exit?

A   Look over your left shoulder to make sure it is safe and get on to the hard shoulder as soon as you can. Use your hazard flashers and get out of the car behind the barrier.

Q   How do I contact the police or breakdown organizations?

A   Use the motorway telephones, which are at one-mile intervals.

Q   Can I use my mobile phone if I have one?

A   Yes, but the police may ask you to use the motorway phone as well, as this confirms exactly where you are.

Q   If I am a lone female driver and break down, do I get any special consideration?

A   Yes, tell the police controller that you are female and alone. They will give you priority assistance.

Q   Are there any special rules about overtaking on motorways?

A   Yes, only do it on the right, and allow plenty of time and room before getting back in. You also need to keep an extra-careful eye on your mirrors to look out for very fast traffic overtaking you.

Q   Which is the overtaking lane on a three-lane motorway?

A   Both lane two and lane three (the middle and right-hand lanes) are overtaking lanes. Only stay in them long enough to get past the slower traffic in lane one (the left-hand lane).

Q   Can I stay in lane two or three for any length of time?

A   You can only stay in an overtaking lane if there is a continual stream of traffic in the lane to your left.

Q   Is there any guideline to say if it is worth pulling back in again before overtaking again?

A   Yes. If no one else is behind you waiting to overtake you, *and* you will need to pull out again within about fifteen seconds, then you can stay out. If anyone wants to get past, and you have space and time, you should pull back in.

Q   If I am driving at 70 mph can I stay in lane three, the right-hand lane?

A   No. The fact you are sticking to the speed limit does not give you the right to tell others they cannot get past you.

Q   But if they are breaking the law, I can help them stay in the legal limits, can't I?

A   No, you are not a police officer. Allow other drivers to make their own decisions.

Q   What do I need to know about changing from one motorway to another?
A   Read the road signs very carefully. Motorway signs are usually very good, but you need to know where you are going. Sometimes you will leave a motorway on the left in order to go right, or on the right in order to go left. This is to allow the various lanes to mix together safely.
Q   What precautions should I take when joining a new motorway?
A   Look out for traffic already on it and adjust your speed to suit, just as if you were joining any motorway.
Q   Do I need to take any special precautions when leaving a motorway for an ordinary road?
A   Yes, the main thing is to keep an eye on your speed. After driving along a motorway at higher speeds, it is sometimes more difficult to adjust to driving at 30 mph or less.

7. After the driving test: driving on your own

Now that you are driving on your own you will have to make all your own decisions. This includes developing a keen sense of vehicle sympathy. Not only will it save you a lot of money if you can detect potential faults and have them corrected early, you can save yourself the embarrassment of breaking down in expensive locations, or being blacklisted by the motoring organizations. Both the RAC and the AA eventually get fed up with being called out to the same drivers and vehicles and make you pay more.

You also need to make decisions about such things as the use of car telephones. Mobile phones are so cheap these days that many people have them in their cars just in case. But if you are tempted to use one in the car, there are only two ways in which you can do this. One is to pull off the road and stop: lay-bys and other places are ideal. The other is to use a proper in-car (hands-free) fixture which means you can talk and listen without taking your hands off the car controls. Nevertheless, even this is not ideal. A hands-free telephone is not a brain-free telephone and as such is still a hazard and therefore illegal if used on the move.

You may also find that once you have your full driving licence you are allowed to drive a whole range of different vehicles all of which can be driven on this licence. For example, if you move some furniture or goods, you can legally drive a fairly large box van. It only needs to be less than 7.5 tonnes (7.4 tons) laden weight, and car hire companies advertise how easy they are to hire. If you do, take someone experienced with you, and get some practice in first; some of those box vans, horseboxes, and similar sized vehicles are simple enough to drive but real pigs to manoeuvre until you have learned their sizes and shapes.

You may also enjoy the thought of driving an off-road vehicle – these are very popular in the King's Road area around Chelsea, which is not the most obvious off-road driving area. They are fun to drive, especially the smaller ones, but if you do decide to take them overland and on to fields and byways, make sure you get some proper training first. A few years ago, a great storm brewed up in a teacup because some drivers managed to roll them over on hills. Training is the answer, and you can be sure that it is not the vehicles that were unstable.

Once you own your own vehicle, regardless of what it is and how much it cost, you will soon learn the value of locking it securely when you leave it, and also hiding any goods away in the boot or out of sight. A good immobilizer can be value for money too. Remember that car thieves will always steal a car or its contents if they really want to: your task is to make it more difficult so that the opportunist thief is less likely to be tempted.

FACT FILE

When you pass your test your days of learning are only just beginning.

You won't always have a teacher to tell you what to do. You have to learn.

Take professional training on any new aspect of driving that worries you.

Read *Ten Important Things Your Driving Instructor Never Taught You*, Peter Russell (Bloomsbury, 1996).

Take additional training as recommended by the Department of Transport for their Pass Plus insurance scheme.

Go on to take advanced driving training. Enjoy the extra skills you will learn.

Take advanced driving tests to prove that you are as good as you want to be.

Q   What is meant by vehicle sympathy?

A   Once you know a car well, you can develop a sense of recognition of its well-being. You can begin to identify unusual noises or sensations.

Q   What do I need to develop a sense of vehicle sympathy?

A   The main need is for interest, and a desire to get to know what the car does, how it does it, and where the weaknesses are.

Q   What is the main purpose of a portable telephone in a motor car?

A   There is no motoring need for a mobile telephone. But they can be helpful for getting messages to and from the driver.

Q   Why should I not use a telephone whilst driving?

A   Apart from being dangerous, it is illegal to use a phone whilst on the move.

Q   What does the law say about car phones?

A   The law requires that you exercise proper control of your vehicle at all times. You cannot do this if you are using a phone. Even if you are not holding it, engaging in a conversation can be distracting.

Q   Can I use my phone on a motorway?

A   No. If you need to use a car or portable phone whilst driving on a motorway you must get off at an exit or service station to use it.

Q   Can I pull on to the hard shoulder to use a portable phone?

A   No; the only time you can use a portable phone on the hard shoulder is if you have broken down and are seeking assistance. Even then you are advised to use the motorway phones.

Q   If I hire a 7.5 tonne (7.4 ton) box van what driving licence do I need?

A   You need a full category B driving licence for a car.

Q   Will I need to have any extra driving test before I drive a larger vehicle?

A   If the total laden weight of the vehicle is less than 7.5 tonnes you will not need to take another test. But you may need some training. If in doubt ask for help.

Q   What other types of vehicle can I drive with my category B driving licence?

A   Your full car driving licence entitles you to drive any motor car or light goods vehicle with up to nine seats, and under the 7.5 tonnes laden weight limit (3.5 tonnes or 3.4 tons unladen).

Q   Can I drive a car fitted with an automatic gearbox?

A   Yes, but the holder of an automatic licence cannot drive a manual-gearbox car unaccompanied until they have passed a test in one.

Q   Do I need a driving licence to drive a 4 × 4 vehicle off-road?

A   If the land is private and capable of being fenced off from the public, a driving licence is not required. But if public access is allowed, you must be licensed, regardless of the type of vehicle being driven.

Q   If I drive off-road does my insurance policy cover me against damage and injury?

A   Check with your insurers. Quite often insurance does not cover you when you are not on public roads.

Q   What driving offences can I be charged with?

A   The range of offences is quite large. The lowest charge is for driving without due care and attention. The most serious is causing death by dangerous driving.

Q   Can I lose my driving licence for any driving offences?

A   Yes. If you break the speed limit by more than 30 mph magistrates are advised to disqualify you automatically. Similarly, for serious traffic offences you can not only lose your licence or be sent to prison, you can also be required to take another driving test or an extended driving test before you can get your licence back.

Q   If I have to take an extended driving test will I also have to take the written examination?

Q   Yes, if you revert to learner driver status you must pass both the written test and the practical test (either the normal test or an extended one), before you can get your licence back.

Q   How can I make sure I never slip back from my good driving habits?

A   Take further training – especially on the subjects contained in the DSA's Pass Plus insurance scheme.

Q   What does the DSA's Pass Plus training offer?

A   It suggests a minimum extra six hours' practical training with a professional instructor after you have passed the practical tests. Those who do this successfully will be able to negotiate special insurance deals.

Q   What subjects are covered in the Pass Plus training programme?

A   Motorways, night driving, dual-carriageway and rural-road driving, bad-weather driving and emphasis on gaining proper safe-driving attitudes. All this leads up to training in defensive-driving techniques.

Q   What is defensive driving?

A   Defensive driving takes advanced driving one stage further. Advanced driving means driving safely and efficiently and making good progress. Defensive driving includes making allowances for other road users' bad behaviour and not letting it get you involved in their incidents.

Q   Finally, how can I pass the new Department of Transport written examination?

A   Study this book, read all the background; learn the Fact Files; understand the answers to all the questions; and you will know more than enough to pass any theoretical driving test.

The Learner Driver Theory Test Paper 3

Thirty-five Questions on the Theoretical Training Syllabus for Learner Drivers

> **Choose the answers nearest to the options given which you think are correct; check your score against the answers shown on the answer page and then work out your score. The minimum acceptable score is 26 but before you consider yourself really ready to take the practical driving test you should score at least 32 out of 35.**
>
> **Where more than one answer is needed, all must be correct to count.**
>
> **Marks scored   /35**

Allow forty minutes for this test. Answer without using any books or assistance.

1   You are driving at the 70 mph speed limit in the outside lane of a busy dual carriageway with two lanes of traffic in each direction. The roads are wet. What should you do if the vehicle behind closes up and hoots at you?
A   Pick up speed to catch up the traffic further ahead.
B   Brake firmly with your left foot to activate the brake-lights.
C   Move back into the left-hand lane when it is safe.

D   Close up on the vehicle ahead and sound your horn too.

A ( )   B ( )   C ( )   D ( )

2   The female driver ahead is going too slowly for you and you wish to overtake. The road has many bends and you cannot see very far ahead. What should you do?
A   Toot your horn lightly at first and then for longer periods.
B   Close the gap so that she can see you well in her mirrors.
C   Overtake briskly, knowing she'll drop back if anyone comes.
D   Drop back and wait until a safe opportunity to pass arises.

A ( )   B ( )   C ( )   D ( )

3   Your car's screen-washer container is empty and you cannot clean your windscreen properly. What should you do?
A   Wait until you get back home in order to fill it up.
B   Stop and ring one of the motoring associations for help.
C   Avoid using the wipers to avoid smearing the screen.
D   Call at the first service station or garage to top up.

A ( )   B ( )   C ( )   D ( )

4   The MOT car test is designed to keep vehicles safe on the roads. At what stage in a vehicle's life is its first MOT Test Certificate needed?
A   All vehicles must have them regardless of their age.
B   When they have covered more than 12,000 miles.
C   If they were first registered three years ago.
D   If they were first registered five years ago.

A ( )   B ( )   C ( )   D ( )

5   Which of the following items are not tested in the Government's MOT test for vehicles?
A   Brakes.
B   Seat-belts.
C   Gearbox and clutch.
D   Windscreen.

A ( )   B ( )   C ( )   D ( )

6   What is the minimum total stopping distance for a motor car travelling at 60 mph on a dry road in good conditions?
A   30 metres (98 feet).
B   45 metres (148 feet).
C   60 metres (197 feet).
D   75 metres (246 feet).

A ( )   B ( )   C ( )   D ( )

7   Braking distances are also dependent upon weather conditions. In heavy rain the surface water will affect tyre grip. What sort of changes can a driver expect to find when braking on wet roads?
A   The front tyres will start to aquaplane.
B   The rear tyres will start to aquaplane.
C   Drivers' reactions times take longer.
D   Total stopping distance is more than doubled.

A ( )   B ( )   C ( )   D ( )

8   What is the minimum amount of alcohol which could be consumed by a male driver, about ten stone in weight, before his driving performance was affected?
A   One pint of shandy.
B   Two pints of brown ale.
C   Three pints of lager.
D   Four single gins.

A ( )   B ( )   C ( )   D ( )

9   At what distance are you required to read a number plate in order to drive a motor vehicle?
A   18.5 metres (61 feet).
B   20.5 metres (67 feet).
C   22 metres (72 feet).
D   30 metres (98 feet).

A ( )   B ( )   C ( )   D ( )

10   All vehicles need a registration document. What is the purpose of this document?
A   To raise funds for building new roads.
B   To enable vehicle checks to be made.

C   To identify the driver of the vehicle.
D   To ensure that all vehicles are taxed.

A ( )   B ( )   C ( )   D ( )

11   Which group of vehicle drivers is most vulnerable to road traffic accidents?
A   New drivers aged 17–23.
B   Drivers aged 24–30.
C   Drivers aged 30–45.
D   Older drivers aged 45–60.

A ( )   B ( )   C ( )   D ( )

12   You wish to overtake a large, high-sided truck on a motorway in heavy driving rain. What is the safest way to do this?
A   Get really close behind before pulling out.
B   Stay in the overtaking lane the whole time.
C   Pull out well behind, and get past relatively quickly.
D   Accelerate really hard and flash your lights.

A ( )   B ( )   C ( )   D ( )

13   You are driving in the left lane in a double queue of slow-moving traffic on a dual carriageway. You see a motor cyclist coming up between the two lanes obviously intent on passing you. What should you do?
A   Close the gap on your right to prevent him getting past you.
B   Drop back from the vehicle ahead to make room for him to pull in.
C   Move into the gutter to give him more room to get past at speed.
D   Close up the gap with the vehicle ahead to prevent him getting in.

A ( )   B ( )   C ( )   D ( )

14   You wish to turn left out from a very narrow junction into a busy main road. Where should you position your vehicle whilst waiting to emerge?
A   Well into the left gutter to enable others to enter your road.
B   Across the centre line to give yourself room to swing out.
C   Centred on your half of the road you are in.
D   Well back from the white give-way lines.

A ( )   B ( )   C ( )   D ( )

15   When driving in fog you need to make sure you are seen and heard by other road users. Which of the following is the safest way to drive?
A   Drive with your vehicle lights on full beam whilst following.
B   Keep the vehicle ahead in sight, but at a safe braking distance.
C   Keep the driver's door open to follow the white line.
D   Sound your horn each time you overtake or turn corners.

A ( )   B ( )   C ( )   D ( )

16   You are waiting to turn right at a set of traffic lights at a busy crossroads. Arrows painted on the road tell oncoming vehicles to pass in front of each other. The vehicle facing you, also waiting to turn right, flashes its headlights. What do you do?
A   Turn right in front of it and wave your hand to say thank you.
B   Beware of traffic coming inside as you drive slowly in front.
C   Remain waiting and flash your lights back at the vehicle.
D   Wait for the lights to go red and then turn right quickly.

A ( )   B ( )   C ( )   D ( )

17   You are moving slowly in a stream of traffic in town. Ahead on your left is a stationary bus with its right indicator flashing. What should you do?
A   Check your mirrors and slow down, then let the bus move out.
B   Overtake quickly and allow the bus to move off behind you.
C   Stop quickly and hold your hand out of the window.
D   Stop immediately and flash your headlights to the bus.

A ( )   B ( )   C ( )   D ( )

18   You are 25 metres (82 feet) from an uncontrolled zebra crossing which has two young children running towards it from your left. Two more children are waiting at the kerb on the other side of the road. What should you do?
A   Continue driving across the crossing.
B   Sound your horn and continue driving.
C   Stop, check your mirrors, and wait.
D   Check your mirrors, give an arm signal, and stop.

A ( )   B ( )   C ( )   D ( )

19 You are driving in a busy residential area. The roads are glistening, and frost and ice has been forecast. What should you do to maximize your safety?

A   Maintain your speed at 30 mph as long as you can.
B   Drop down a gear and keep your speed down.
C   Practise your skid control on some quieter roads.
D   Be prepared to slow down without using the brakes.

A ( )   B ( )   C ( )   D ( )

20 You are driving on a dark, wintry night on narrow, winding country lanes with no street lighting. As you approach each bend which TWO of the following would make it easier for you and any other road users?

A   Moving across to the centre of the road on right bends.
B   Sounding your horn each time your visibility ahead decreases.
C   Driving on main beam unless you see other traffic ahead.
D   Adjusting your speed to suit the road and traffic conditions.

A ( )   B ( )   C ( )   D ( )

21 You are in a large saloon car, towing a two-wheeled caravan. What is the speed limit whilst you are on a motorway?

A   50 mph.
B   60 mph.
C   50 mph at night and 60 mph in daylight.
D   70 mph.

A ( )   B ( )   C ( )   D ( )

22 Vehicles and their contents are always at risk from thieves. Which TWO of these will help keep your vehicle and contents safer?

A   Keeping goods and parcels covered up on the back seat?
B   Having all the windows etched with the registration number.
C   Keeping all goods and parcels locked in the boot.
D   Parking in multi-storey car parks.

A ( )   B ( )   C ( )   D ( )

23   You are parking your motor car at night in a city back street. The street lights are lit and no parking restrictions exist. Which TWO of the following would be illegal?
A   Parking on the correct side of the road without lights.
B   Parking on the wrong side of the road with side lights on.
C   Parking closer than 10 metres (33 feet) from a junction without lights.
D   Parking more than 20 metres (66 feet) from a junction without lights.

A ( )   B ( )   C ( )   D ( )

24   The Highway Code advises where you may or may not over-take. Which of the following would *not* be a legal place to overtake?
A   In the left lane in a one-way street.
B   In lanes around a roundabout.
C   In the outside lane 50 metres (164 feet) from a pedestrian crossing.
D   When crossing double white lines with the solid line nearest you.

A ( )   B ( )   C ( )   D ( )

25   Which of the following vehicles and road users are legally allowed to drive on motorways?
A   Motor cars towing caravans driven by learner drivers.
B   Large Goods Vehicles driven by learner drivers.
C   Motor cycles ridden by learner riders.
D   Tractors driven by learner drivers.

A ( )   B ( )   C ( )   D ( )

26   What is the largest single cause of road traffic accidents?
A   Drivers overtaking unsafely.
B   Drivers following too closely behind other vehicles.
C   Excessive alcohol consumption by drivers.
D   Pedestrians crossing roads other than at crossings.

A ( )   B ( )   C ( )   D ( )

27   You discover you are travelling in the wrong direction. Which of these is the safest way to turn back?
A   Find somewhere to do a three-point turn.
B   Reverse into a road on the left and then turn right.
C   Find somewhere to reverse on the right and then turn left.
D   Find a roundabout, or turn off and go round the block.

A ( )   B ( )   C ( )   D ( )

28   Shapes and colours are used to indicate different types of road sign. The purpose of a red circle generally indicates which of the following?
A   Warning sign.
B   Prohibitory sign.
C   Mandatory sign.
D   Information sign.

A ( )   B ( )   C ( )   D ( )

29   You know when the national speed limit of 60 mph is in force by which of the following?
A   The absence of yellow lines at the kerbside.
B   The presence of street lights in a residential area.
C   Single carriageways with no lights or signs showing.
D   Speed limit camera warning signs.

A ( )   B ( )   C ( )   D ( )

30   Your car ran into the back of another which stopped suddenly when approaching a roundabout. Considerable damage was caused to both vehicles, but no one was hurt. What must you do?
A   Exchange details of drivers, owners, and insurance.
B   Call the police immediately in order to make a statement.
C   Report to a police station within seven days with all details.
D   Wait at the scene of the accident until the police arrive.

A ( )   B ( )   C ( )   D ( )

31   You are driving on a single carriageway road. 200 metres (218 yards) ahead two trucks are coming towards you. One of them pulls out on to your side of the road to overtake the other. What should you do?

A Maintain your speed for the present.
B Check your mirrors and slow down.
C Brake and expect to stop.
D Flash your lights to warn the truck drivers.

A ( )   B ( )   C ( )   D ( )

32 When you break down on a country road you are advised to place a warning triangle on the hard shoulder some distance behind your vehicle. What is the recommended distance?
A 15 metres (49 feet).
B 25 metres (82 feet).
C 50 metres (164 feet).
D 100 metres (109 yards).

A ( )   B ( )   C ( )   D ( )

33 You are first to arrive at the scene of a serious multiple vehicle accident. A driver has just called the emergency services, but there are a number of injured. Which of the following is your major priority?
A Giving drinks and cigarettes to those who want them.
B Getting all of the injured out of their vehicles.
C Moving all the vehicles off the road.
D Making sure all engines are switched off.

A ( )   B ( )   C ( )   D ( )

34 As a driver of a vehicle you are required to give way to pedestrians at certain times and places. At which of the following would you normally be willing to take priority?
A Whilst driving across the pavement when leaving your house.
B When they are waiting to cross the road at a zebra crossing.
C When a policeman is controlling the traffic at a zebra crossing.
D When turning left into a side road with pedestrians crossing it.

A ( )   B ( )   C ( )   D ( )

35 You have just passed your driving test in a motor car and you want to borrow your father's 7.5 tonne (7.4 ton) box van to move some furniture. What should you do?

A   Avoid driving it at more than 30 mph.
B   Take another driving test for this category of vehicle.
C   Have some practice at driving and parking the vehicle.
D   Make sure you have a qualified driver sitting with you.

A ( )   B ( )   C ( )   D ( )

The Learner Driver Theory Test – Answer Sheet Paper 3

1		2		3		4		5	
A	☐	A	☐	A	☐	A	☐	A	☐
B	☐	B	☐	B	☐	B	☐	B	☐
C	X	C	☐	C	☐	C	X	C	X
D	☐	D	X	D	X	D	☐	D	☐

6		7		8		9		10	
A	☐	A	☐	A	X	A	☐	A	☐
B	☐	B	☐	B	☐	B	X	B	X
C	☐	C	☐	C	☐	C	☐	C	☐
D	X	D	X	D	☐	D	☐	D	☐

11		12		13		14		15	
A	X	A	☐	A	☐	A	☐	A	☐
B	☐	B	☐	B	X	B	☐	B	X
C	☐	C	X	C	☐	C	X	C	☐
D	☐	D	☐	D	☐	D	☐	D	☐

16		17		18		19		20	
A	☐	A	X	A	☐	A	☐	A	☐
B	X	B	☐	B	☐	B	X	B	☐
C	☐	C	☐	C	☐	C	☐	C	X
D	☐	D	☐	D	X	D	☐	D	X

21		22		23		24		25	
A	☐	A	☐	A	☐	A	☐	A	☐
B	X	B	X	B	X	B	☐	B	X
C	☐	C	X	C	X	C	☐	C	☐
D	☐	D	☐	D	☐	D	X	D	☐

26		27		28		29		30	
A	☐	A	☐	A	☐	A	☐	A	X
B	X	B	☐	B	X	B	☐	B	☐
C	☐	C	☐	C	☐	C	X	C	☐
D	☐	D	X	D	☐	D	☐	D	☐

31		32		33		34		35	
A	☐	A	☐	A	☐	A	☐	A	☐
B	X	B	☐	B	☐	B	☐	B	☐
C	☐	C	X	C	☐	C	X	C	X
D	☐	D	☐	D	X	D	☐	D	☐

Appendix: How the written driving test is composed

The individual headings of the question paper ranges are:

1. *Alertness*
Concentration, anticipation, observation, awareness, distraction, and boredom and their effect on drivers.

2%

2. *Driver attitude to other road users*
Consideration, following too close, courtesy, and priority.

4%

3. *Weather and road conditions*
Safety margins, and the effect of weather and road surface conditions, visibility.

8%

4. *Impairment*
The effect of alcohol, fatigue, medication, drugs, stress, ill health, ageing, sensory impairment (including eyesight), regulations.

6%

5. *Perception*
Information processing, attention, scanning, identification of hazards, time to detect hazards, fixation, interpretation.

(Combined weighting with 'Judgement' below)

6. *Judgement and decision taking*
Appropriate action, interpretation, reaction time, speed and distance.

20%

7. *Other road users*
Elderly drivers, motor cyclists, new drivers, vulnerable road users, children, pedestrians, cyclists, disabled people, those with lack of traffic experience, conspicuity.

10%

8. *Other vehicle handling*
Motor cycles, lorries, buses: manoeuvrability, field of view, braking distances, acceleration, performance, winds and weather, road surface, spray.

4%

9. *Own vehicle handling*
The effects of weather, road conditions, time of day, lighting, calming, speed.

6%

10. *Roads and regulations – motorways*
Limitations on motorways, speed limits, lane discipline, parking, lighting.

4%

11. *Roads and regulations – other roads*
Limitations on other types of roads, speed limits, parking clearways, lighting.

6%

12. *Signs and signals*
Road traffic regulations regarding road signs, markings, signals, rights of way, and speed limits.

12%

13. *Documents*
Rules concerning administrative documents required for the use of vehicles.

2%

14. *Accident handling*
Use of first-aid kits and other first-aid precautions, setting warning devices, and raising the alarm, police reporting procedures, witness responsibilities, regulations.

4%

15. *Vehicle loading*
Safety factors concerning vehicles and persons carried, stability, towing, regulations.

2%

16. *Accident risk*
Relative risk for different road-user groups, situations and contexts, impairment, road types, speed, and speed in relation to the severity of accidents.

4%

17. *Vehicle defects, safety equipment, and the environment*
(a) Mechanical faults and defects, detection and understanding of the implications; or
(b) Use of safety equipment, seat-belts, child seats, etc; or
(c) Fuel consumption, emissions, pollution (including noise) regulations.

6%

Questions will be asked from one area only of Section 17 (a), (b) or (c) above.

The proportions of questions will be based on percentages shown at the end of each section.